HIGH SCHOOL BOUND

The ULTIMATE guide for high school success and survival!

By Martin J. Spethman
Illustrated by Chuck Klein

Westgate Publishing & Entertainment, Inc.

This book is printed on chlorine free recycled paper.

Cover design and composition by Westgate Publishing & Entertainment, Inc. Terri Terraferma.

For information concerning this publication and discount quantity purchases contact: Westgate Publishing & Entertainment, Inc. 260 Crandon Blvd. Suite 32-109 Key Biscayne, Florida 33149 Phone (305) 361-6862 or 800-345-0096.

ISBN number: 0-9633598-1-9

Printed in the USA.

ABOUT THE AUTHOR:

Martin J. Spethman: Graduated from kindergarten, elementary school, middle school, high school and even college. He is also the author of <u>How to get into and graduate from college in 4 years with good grades, a useful major, a lot of knowledge, a little debt, great friends, happy parents, maximum party attendance, minimal weight gain, decent habits, fewer hassles, a career goal, and a super attitude, all while remaining extremely cool!</u>

ABOUT THE EDITORS:

Bonnie J. Pryor: has been a teacher and administrator for Cathedral elementary and secondary schools in Omaha, Nebraska since 1956. She was the President of NCEA Department of Elementary Schools Executive Committee from 1990 - 1993. She received the 1985 National Distinguished Principal Award and the 1986 National Exemplary School Award from the United States Department of Education. In 1991 she received the Outstanding Teacher/Administrator of Religious Education Award. In 1993 she was awarded the YWCA Outstanding Educator in the City of Omaha, Nebraska.

Gregory J. Glenn: Received his B.A. from Santa Clara University and his Masters from the University of Notre Dame. He has been the Admissions Director at Creighton Prep School in Omaha, Nebraska for 6 years. He also has been a teacher of World, U.S. and European history for 18 years. He was the past Chairman of the Social Studies Department and twice selected Outstanding Teacher of the Year (1981 & 1989).

ABOUT THE ILLUSTRATOR:

Chuck Klein: Graduated from the Art Institute in Fort Lauderdale, Florida. He is a freelance illustrator and does work for clients in Miami, New York and Los Angeles. He specializes in illustrations and T.V. storyboards.

I would like to thank the following people who have contributed their time and expertise to this book: Spethman Family Reviewers, Tom Dethlefs, Tom Rohling, Kam Kadivar, Emily Moore, and Kay K. Hale for her excellent review on Library survival.

I would also like to thank the following counseling professionals who have contributed their time and expertise to this book:

Laurel Sutton

Kathy Hews

Marian Camel R.S.M.

Betsy Morrison

Kim Burger

Sharon Lewis

Table of Contents

CONGRATULATIONS, you are about to graduate! This is your last year before you attend the ultimate cool school known as High School. Although you will be saying good-bye to recess, study periods, difficult teachers, friends, homework and skateland parties, you will be saying hello to free periods, study halls, more teachers, more friends, more parties and much more homework.

SO TELL US HOW YOU FEEL ABOUT GOING TO HIGH SCHOOL?

❏ It's great   ❏ Haven't thought about it much

❏ I am not sure   ❏ I'd rather not

❏ I am nervous   ❏ All of the above

Your own feelings please _ _ _ _ _ _ _ _ _ _ _ _ _

_ _

_ _

_ _

_ _

AND WHAT ARE YOUR BIGGEST CONCERNS ABOUT GOING TO HIGH SCHOOL?

- ❏ Will I get good grades?
- ❏ Will I be able to play the sport I like?
- ❏ Fitting in
- ❏ Fitting in my new clothes
- ❏ Fitting in my old clothes
- ❏ Getting into the school I want
- ❏ Getting involved in drugs
- ❏ Hanging out with the wrong crowd
- ❏ Safety
- ❏ The first day
- ❏ School size
- ❏ Money
- ❏ Homework
- ❏ Hard classes
- ❏ Will I have a boyfriend?
- ❏ Will I have a girlfriend?
- ❏ Will I have friends?
- ❏ Will my dog miss me while I'm at school?
- ❏ What will I eat for lunch?
- ❏ Getting lost
- ❏ Will people like me?
- ❏ Will the teachers be nice?
- ❏ Will the teachers be hard?
- ❏ Getting a bad reputation
- ❏ Will I be considered a nerd?
- ❏ Will I be popular?
- ❏ Will I ever learn how to drive?
- ❏ Will my braces bother me?
- ❏ Tests
- ❏ Going to the same school as my sister or brother
- ❏ Peer pressure
- ❏ Bullies
- ❏ Bulliettes (female bullies)
- ❏ Lockers
- ❏ Waking up earlier
- ❏ Being the youngest on campus
- ❏ Not being able to watch TV as much

Please add your own here: _ _ _ _ _ _ _ _ _ _ _ _ _ _ _ _ _ _ _

_ _

_ _

_ _

So, what should be your biggest concern about going to high school? How about, getting the most out of every day, every class, every subject, every teacher, every practice, every game, and every time you are with your friends and family?! High school is going to be much more than just new classrooms, in a new school with new teachers. You are going to have sports, speech, a school newspaper, and drama clubs. You are going to have new friends, new parties, new teachers, new classrooms, new hallways, and even your first or at least new lockers. You are going to have new schedules, hear new music, and discuss new ideas. Each one of you can get as much out of high school as you put into it! A great way to accomplish this is by going to high school prepared. **I would say you are off to a great start by reading and using this book!**

How should you use this book? Well, use it anyway you want. Just use it! Throw it in your back pack. Throw it at your little brother or sister. Fill it out; Read it once; Read it twice; Read it out loud; Just read it! Use this book as your personal high school preparation note-book. Oh, by the way, there is a section in the back of the book called "Just for Parents" (Page 139). You will want to make sure your parents read this. Tell them they have to read it or they are grounded. Go ahead and tell them now.

So, what is the best way to get the most out of high school? Where should we start? How about making some goals for ourselves? O.K. Our first goal is to turn the page.

GOALS

Chapter 1

Goals are the greatest! Everyone has his or her own goals. It is important from time to time to set goals for yourself. It really helps to list your goals on paper and think about how you plan to accomplish them. A person's goals will change from time to time and be replaced by new goals. What is important is to try to take steps to achieve them. For example, today your goal should be to read this chapter and write down some goals.

Let's take a few minutes and list some of the goals you have now and the steps needed to accomplish them.

Goals	Steps to take to achieve goal	Date of first step	Date Completed
Read High School Bound by Martin J. Spethman.	Start reading book	May 3, 99	June 1st, 99
Improve dribbling soccer ball.	Practice 20 minutes every day after school	May 10, 99	June 10th, 99

It is important you occasionally write down your goals and the steps needed to accomplish them. Here is another chart which can be used in the future to write down your goals. Make a copy of it and start your own personal "goal booklet".

Goals	Steps to take to achieve goal	Date of first step	Date Completed
Goal #1			
Goal #2			
Goal #3			
Goal #4			

Even if you do not completely accomplish your goals, it is important to try! The greatest thing about goals is that just by trying to reach a goal, you end up improving yourself tremendously!

GETTING PREPARED FOR HIGH SCHOOL

Your first step to prepare for high school is to complete grade school, middle school or junior high. Get as much out of your last year as possible. Continue to study hard, practice hard and enjoy your friends. Although you might be a little tired of school by now, or maybe even so sick of school you want to_____(fill in your own), it is necessary to continue to pay attention in your classes and do your homework.

It is very important that you have hopefully learned what you were supposed to learn in grade school, middle school or junior high. High school does not get any easier. Do not be afraid to ask for help. You may be the only one who knows you are having a problem in a particular area. If you are having problems in any particular area of school, take action now! Talk to your parents and teachers and ask them what can be done to help you with a subject or acquire the skills necessary for high school.

WHAT TO DO IF YOU NEED HELP IN A PARTICULAR AREA OR SUBJECT.

If you decide you need help in any subject, check with your teachers and parents on how you can improve your skills in that particular area. For example, if you think you read too slowly or do not remember what you read, then you need to work on your reading speed and comprehension. In order to improve, you should plan on reading 4 books a month from now until high school starts and look into a reading course. Your local library has book clubs to help with reading, and your local schools should offer reading courses. A great place to improve your knowledge in certain subjects is summer school. I know what you are saying, *"More school? What are you, nuts?"* Actually, summer school is not so bad, because you can focus on just the subject that needs improving. Or maybe just some independent reading or activities will bring your skills up to where they should be. By improving your skills now, you will make high school much easier. (Besides, you'll be taking classes, workshops and seminars the rest of your life.)

How do you find out what areas need improving? Here are a few questions which will help you think about your **STUDY SKILLS:**

Yes	No	STUDY SKILLS
❑	❑	Can I read quickly and remember what I have read?
❑	❑	Can I write and spell correctly? Grammar and composition?
❑	❑	Can I write a speech, term paper, and book review?
❑	❑	Can I add, subtract, divide, and multiply? Do I understand math story problems?
❑	❑	Am I good in social studies?
❑	❑	Am I good in sciences?
❑	❑	How are my scores on standardized exams?
❑	❑	Can I use a computer?
❑	❑	Do I know how to use a library to get research material?
❑	❑	Do I know how to take lecture notes for a class?
❑	❑	Do I know how to take notes from my textbooks?
❑	❑	Do I know how to write a schedule for my various activities?
❑	❑	Are my study skills good?
❑	❑	Do I like school and going to classes?
❑	❑	Am I good at organizing and keeping track of homework?
❑	❑	Do I get extremely nervous before tests?
❑	❑	Do I have trouble concentrating on school?
❑	❑	Do I daydream in class?

Now let's fill out your own **LEARNING PROGRESS CHART**. Make sure you discuss it with your parents and teachers. Ask them what skills or subjects they think you need to improve.

LEARNING PROGRESS CHART

Area or Subject that needs improvement	What will I do to improve myself (Be specific)
Reading. I read too slowly.	Read 4 books a month and take a reading course.
I do not take useful notes in class.	Talk to teachers after a few classes about reviewing notes and check on how my notes could be improved.

Now being prepared for high school does not just mean being prepared in your study skills and school subjects. It means being ready personally for high school.

Let's see what areas you might want to improve. Here are a few questions which will help you think about your **personal living skills**:

Yes	No	PERSONAL LIVING SKILLS
❑	❑	Do I feel confident in my ability to do or try something new?
❑	❑	Am I happy with my personality?
❑	❑	Am I happy with how I look?
❑	❑	Are there things about me I would like to change?
❑	❑	Can I list 3 things I like about myself?
❑	❑	When someone makes me mad, do I handle it in a nice way?
❑	❑	Do I treat others like I want to be treated?
❑	❑	Am I always honest with people?
❑	❑	Do I listen considerately to others?
❑	❑	Does my family talk to each other about problems?
❑	❑	Is there something bothering me that I have not told anyone about?
❑	❑	Do I usually look for negative things in people?
❑	❑	Do I usually look for positive things in people?
❑	❑	Do I worry about a lot of things?
❑	❑	Do I enjoy being by myself occasionally?
❑	❑	Do I exercise regularly?
❑	❑	Am I happy with the way my friends treat me?
❑	❑	Am I always depressed?
❑	❑	Do I know the facts about drugs such as pot and cocaine?
❑	❑	Do I know the facts about sex?
❑	❑	Can I handle peer pressure and always make my own decisions?

Now let's fill out your own **PERSONAL PROGRESS CHART.** If you want to discuss it with your parents, then go ahead. If you want to keep it to yourself, that is fine too.

PERSONAL PROGRESS CHART

Area or topic that needs improvement	What will I do to improve myself (Be specific)
I do not feel confident trying new things.	Take up a challenging hobby or do something I would really like to do and practice. Maybe dance or karate lessons.
I am not sure I really know about drugs.	Ask counselor at school to give me information, ask teacher to have a drug class. Talk to parents about having a discussion about drugs, NOT A LECTURE! and what I should know.

WHAT TO DO IF YOU NEED HELP

If you feel you need work in any of the areas listed above, then you should talk to your parents, teachers or your school counselor about where to get help. If you do not feel you can talk to your parent or parents, check with your teachers and/or school counselors. Do not be afraid or worried about talking to people about problems you are having. Talking about problems will help you straighten them out!

PEOPLE TO TALK TO

Let's make a list of the people who are going to help you with your high school preparation activities. This includes people who can help you with school subjects, people who are going to help you learn about your potential high school, and also people who can help you with problems you are having. Let's list them now:

	Name:
Parents	
Brothers	
Sisters	
Cousins	
Counselors	
Teachers	
Friends	
Neighbors	
Students currently attending the school where you want to go:	
Counselors/teachers and/or coaches of potential high school:	
Pets	

SO WHAT SHOULD YOUR PARENT(S) DO TO HELP YOU PREPARE FOR HIGH SCHOOL?

They should buy you a new car and stereo and give you $500 a week allowance. You wish! Preparing for high school is not something you can do alone. There are a few things you want to let your parents and teachers handle. Make sure your parent(s) have the "Just for Parents" chapter (page 139) of this book and are reading it. Either share the book with them or just rip out Chapter 19 and give it to them.

WHICH HIGH SCHOOL DO YOU WANT TO ATTEND?

By now you may already know where you want to go to high school or at least have it narrowed down to a few choices. It is important to try to visit potential high schools. Go to the school for the day. Most high schools have an "Open House". Usually these are held several times a year, for high school bound students. These are great opportunities to talk to teachers, coaches, current students, and to check out the campus and classrooms. Some high schools also will come to your school and recruit.

HERE ARE SOME QUESTIONS YOU SHOULD ASK YOUR FUTURE HIGH SCHOOL TEACHERS, RECRUITERS OR OTHER STUDENTS.

1. What do I need to remember about high school that most freshmen forget?

2. How much time does_____(sport or activity) take after school?

3. What do _____(school name) students usually do for fun?

4. What interesting programs does your high school offer, such as retreats, clubs, environmental awareness days, etc..?

5. What makes _____(school name) different than other high schools?

6. What scholarships or financial aid packages are available?

Add other questions here which you are curious about:

7. _____

8. _____

9. _____

10. _____

11. _____

Here is a **HIGH SCHOOL PREPARATION CHART** to help you keep track of information. If you have already decided where you are going, use the chart to organize your material.

HIGH SCHOOL PREPARATION CHART:

	Choice #1	Choice #2
Name High school choices (2)		
Tuition	$	$
Have talked to my parents about choices.	Yes No	Yes No
Have spoken to a counselor or teacher about choices.	Y N	Y N
Have information on schools.	Y N	Y N
Have checked with my parents to make sure they have all paperwork necessary to enroll me.	Y N	Y N
High schools open house: School: Date: Time:		
Have spoken to students and friends who go there.	Y N	Y N
Have met a few of the high school teachers.	Y N	Y N
Have talked to coach(s) of sport(s)/activity in which I want to participate.	Y N	Y N
Have visited the campus.	Y N	Y N
Have discussed tuition with parents.	Y N	Y N
I think I am going to go to		

During your last year of grade school, middle school, or junior high, besides having fun, you will want to work to improve both your educational and personal skills. Before you know it, your last day of school will arrive and it will be time to graduate to the ultimate cool school we call High School. So what should you do on your last day of grade school, middle school or junior high?

OTHER THINGS I SHOULD DO TO PREPARE FOR HIGH SCHOOL.

_____

_____

_____

_____

_____

_____

_____

Chapter 3

YOUR LAST DAY OF ELEMENTARY SCHOOL, MIDDLE SCHOOL, OR JUNIOR HIGH

Yes, it is your last day of grade school, middle school, or junior high; No more school, no more teachers, no more staying after school, and no more homework! Well what are you doing? Run, ride, skate, or surf for your life, summer is here!!!!!!!!!!! What? You want to stay in school another year? Wow, that is radical. If you want to stay, that is fine, but for those normal people, here are a few things you should do on or before your last day of school.

1. THANK YOUR TEACHERS: What.....Yes, believe it or not, on your last day you should do one thing before you head off into the summer sunset. You should thank your teachers for teaching you. Tell all of your teachers thank-you even if you do not want to. Thank them for teaching you. Thank them for answering your many questions. Thank them for sharing their time with you. Even thank them for giving you homework and making you stay after school on occasion. However, you do not have to thank them for giving you difficult math story problems. There is no excuse for that torture.

2. THANK YOUR PARENTS OR PARENT: Thank them for all the help they gave you throughout grade school, middle school or junior high. Thank them for rides to school. Thank them for school clothes. Thank them for letting you stay out later. Thank them for the new stereo, T.V., clothes and private phone they are going to buy you for graduation. Maybe you'll catch them off guard and they will actually go buy you these things. Yeah right!

3. THANK YOUR BROTHERS AND SISTERS: Thank them for being around and putting up with you at times. In fact, let them borrow all of your stuff and watch their favorite TV show whenever they want. Also, let them use the phone first and hang out with you and your friends. O.k. so maybe not...

4. TAKE CARE OF ANY UNFINISHED BUSINESS: There are a lot of things you should take with you from grade school, middle school or junior high to high school. Bad feelings or grudges should not be one of them. If you have been fighting with someone or have bad feelings toward a teacher, friend or another student, now is the time to make peace. Say whatever you think needs to be said to this person, before you go. Make your peace and whatever you do, do not take any grudges or bad feelings with you. If you are not sure what to say to them, try this:

> "I know we have not always seen eye to eye on things, but I want you to know I want to leave school thinking we can be friends. If I did or said anything which hurt your feelings, I am sorry, and I hope you feel the same way."

> or

> "I'm happy we went to school together, but I did not like when you did... or said.... I just wanted to say that, and I hope we can be friends."

Chances are very good with this approach you will solve whatever the problem was and move on to high school without any unfinished business.

5. GET YOUR FRIENDS' ADDRESSES AND PHONE NUMBERS: There is a handy address book right in the back of this book, so make sure you get all of your classmates, addresses and phone numbers. It's important to get

numbers from every student in your class, not just the people you hang around. Some people call this networking, we can just call it hanging out. Also tell your friends to leave you a note. You will get a kick out of it when you are 4000 years old and talking about grade, middle school or junior high. Also, get a picture or two. It is true during high school you will loose touch with some of your grade school, middle

school or junior high friends. Some will attend other high schools and some of you will just drift apart. Try to keep old friends while meeting new ones.

6. GET BUSY: Now, believe it or not, everyone feels a little sad when their last day of grade school arrives. This is normal and cool! Do not worry. You can still stay in touch and see all of your friends. You can even do some of your old homework assignments. Actually, I do not think anyone will be that sad! The best way to get over this sadness is to get busy and since

OTHER THINGS I NEED TO DO ON MY LAST DAY OF SCHOOL.

- -

- -

- -

- -

- -

- -

- -

Chapter 4

So What Should I Do All Summer?

Summer is here and it's time for staying out late, hanging out by the pool, working and (fill in your own please)

_____

_____

_____!

There are a million things you can do during your summer before high school, so let's talk about a few besides drinking soda, eating pizza for breakfast, lunch, and dinner, and getting sunburned in between trips to the mall.

Yes, believe it or not, more school, as in summer school, is a great way to spend part of your summer. Check to see if your future high school offers any courses you might be interested in taking. Taking a class at your new high school will not only keep your brain active, it will also help you become familiar with the campus and meet a few people. Computer courses or study skill courses are always good choices.

WHAT TO TAKE IN SUMMER SCHOOL

Subject	School	Dates/Days	Time
1.			
2.			
3.			

If you are interested in playing a sport in high school or participating in any extracurricular activity, there are three words to remember for the summer, **PRACTICE, PRACTICE, AND PRACTICE!!** You can sharpen your skills by practicing. Take the time and do it everyday. Practice dribbling a basketball, soccer ball, dancing, running, throwing, playing the guitar, or piano. High school sports and activities are very competitive and although there will be a lot of students trying out for the teams, not everyone takes advantage of the summer to improve their skills.

Your prospective high school might have a sports camp or tournament you can compete in during the summer. Look into summer leagues or camps. Look into more lessons if you are playing a musical instrument. If you want to watch MTV, then skip practice and watch it; if you want to be on MTV someday, then go to practice.

SPORTS AND HOBBIES TO PRACTICE

Sport and/ or activity	Days	Time/How long	Particular skills
Soccer	Tues-Sun	9:00-10:00am	Dribbling, juggling ball, shooting with left foot
Play piano	Mon-Fri	3:00-4:00pm	Learn new song

Go to an event or field trip once a month. The zoo, concerts, museums, ball games, day camps, ballets, dog shows, horse shows, state parks for hiking and camping, car shows, anything. Take advantage of any activity to learn something new. Anytime you want to go somewhere worthwhile and your parents are not being cooperative, just tell them it is really an educational field trip, a necessary part of your quest for knowledge, and it will help you become a better person if they let you go. They will not be able to argue with this, hopefully.

FIELD TRIPS I WANT TO GO ON

Field Trip	Date	Where
Natural Science Museum	Sept. 30th	
Pearl Jam Concert	Oct. 5th	Civic Auditorium

If you have never attended a camp before, look into various camps. As we mentioned above, sport camps are great ways to improve your skills over the summer. But there are all sorts of other camps you can attend, not only as a camper but maybe as a junior counselor.

CAMPS TO LOOK INTO

Almost everybody needs to work, right? You should start a month or two before school is out and think about a summer job. The paper, under the classified employment section, is a great place to find leads on jobs. However, when you are younger than 16, jobs such as mowing lawns, babysitting, dog walking, painting or chores around the house are perfect options. If there is any particular place where you would like to work, simply have your parents take you there, neatly dressed of course, and ask for the manager or person responsible for hiring. See if they have any openings or are hiring in the near future. You never know until you ask. Let's list some potential summer jobs for you to check out: (See Chapter 14 on Work)

POTENTIAL PART TIME JOB CHART.

Employer Phone	Contact	Interview/ Fill out application	Pay Hours/ Days	Job Descript.	What I can learn
Burger King 361-6862	Mr. Chase 3:30	Monday May 1	$5/hr 3-9	french fry maker	food service cooking french fries
Dog Kennel 361-8623	Mr. Homan May 3	Sat & Sun	$5/hr	Care for dogs	Dog Care, clean kennels, training dogs

If you have a particular hobby or interest, look for jobs in that area. If you like music, get a job at a record shop. If you like animals, get a job at a zoo or kennel. You might even want to start your own business such as a lawn service or washing cars or babysitting. List some jobs you could do on your own.

START YOUR OWN BUSINESS:

Type of business	Potential Customers	Information Needed	Supplies	Pay
Babysitting	Neighbors, cousins, sister	Learn first aid, games	-	$5/hr
Lawn Service	Neighbors	Lawn Care Book How much gas/oil used per yard...	Mower, trimmers bags	$15/ lawn
Tutoring	Neighbors, cousins	Old school book review 5th grade math	-	$5/hr

One of the best habits you can have is to read books. By reading books, especially right before high school begins, you are going to make your high school days much easier. Reading several books over the summer will increase your reading speed and comprehension and allow you to finish homework (and there will be plenty of it) faster in high school. Try to read at least 12 books over the summer. This book is one, so hey, you are down to eleven. And "Scummy monster truck, crash your head magazine" doesn't count. Neither does "Loves drippy dreamboat with long hair and muscles under an oak tree".

BOOKS TO READ OVER THE SUMMER

1. *High School Bound by Martin J. Spethman*	✔
2.	❑
3.	❑
4.	❑
5.	❑
6.	❑
7.	❑
8.	❑
9.	❑
10.	❑
11.	❑
12.	❑

To get the most out of your summer, make a summer activities schedule! Check out Chapter 8 on Scheduling and then make a summer schedule in order to squeeze the most fun into June, July, and August.

One summer activity you definitely want to do before high school starts is to organize your room. So let's check out Chapter 5.

ORGANIZING YOUR ROOM

Before your first day of high school, it is important to organize your room. Now, some of you have your own room and some share a room with your wonderful, intelligent, caring, clean, demon-like, dirty, monster-like brothers and sisters.

A high school student's room is important. You need a place where you can read and study privately. Other members of the household should know this and knock before entering the room. You need to speak to your parents about some things you will need for your room. Let your parent(s) know you need to make a few changes in your room to get ready for high school. It is important you have a place to study and organize your school materials. For example, it could be a corner of your bedroom where you set up a desk and put up a bulletin board.

YOU WILL NEED THE FOLLOWING:

- ❏ Desk or table with comfortable chair. (set up in your study area).
- ❏ Big wall or desk calendar, to help you keep track of activities and homework. (see Chapter 8 on Scheduling).
- ❏ Notebooks, pens, pencils, ruler.
- ❏ File cabinet/desk organizer or paper holder: Have a separate file for each subject.
- ❏ Optional: Car, stereo, TV, new wardrobe, waterbed, a puppy, moped, subscription to Seventeen, Sports Illustrated.
- ❏ List other items you need for high school: _ _ _ _ _ _ _ _ _ _ _ _ _ _ _
  _
  _

- ❏ Calculator
- ❏ Dictionary and Thesaurus
- ❏ Atlas
- ❏ Desk lamp
- ❏ Alarm clock
- ❏ Wrist watch
- ❏ Back pack
- ❏ Computer

Use this space below to draw the floor plan for your **NEW ULTRA-COOL HIGH SCHOOL ROOM.**

After getting the necessary supplies, start both a personal file and a school file. These can be stored in your desk drawer or a file cabinet. You can keep your homework, school materials, and papers in your school file(s). You can keep items such as your bank savings account information, your diary and your love letters in your personal files(s).

Family Study Time ("FST")

It is important you not only organize your room for high school but also your house.

Discuss with your parent(s) your schedule and establish a study time for the whole family. This means every day whether it is right after school or right after dinner, you will have at least an hour or two of quiet, no TV, no phone calls, study time. Don't worry, you can schedule it around your favorite TV show if you want. You can wait to plan your family study time after you have been in high school a week and see what the best time is, considering any practices, homework load, and yes, even TV shows. Make sure you discuss and organize with your brothers and sisters setting up an FST. (**Remember, you can also study during times that are not FST.**)

Places to Organize

Kitchens are the central room for most families. Your family probably already has some rules for the kitchen. If not, here are two key habits to make life easier on everybody in your house, especially your mom. Always take your own dishes over to the sink after meals and put them in the dish washer or clean them. If you take your lunch to school, always make it the night before. If your parents are working at night and you have to cook for yourself, try to organize meals once a week with them. Every Sunday, decide what you will have for dinner every day the next week. Make sure they shop so you have healthy, easy meals to make. Check out your local bookstore for a good cookbook for the active high school student. In addition, believe it or not, a good set of tup-a-ware is a must for the active high schooler. This way you can make things in large quantities and then store it, using it all week.

The kitchen is the key room in the house not only because it is where you eat, but also it usually serves as the communications center. Designate a place, either on the refrigerator or a bulletin board, usually by a phone, where all family members can leave notes. In high school, you are going to find yourself going to various activities. Get in the habit of always leaving a note when you go somewhere, with a phone number and the time you think you will be back. **Parents like this and it almost always results in your parents giving you more freedom because you always tell them where** you are, how you can be reached, and when you will be back..

Bathrooms are another hot spot, especially since almost all families have fewer bathrooms than they do people living in the house. Make sure you discuss and decide on who uses what bathroom and when, especially in the morning. Major wars can be started by trying to use the bathroom at the wrong time. A good tip to save bathroom time is for the girls in the house to take their blow dryers and curling irons to their bedrooms after their showers and fix their hair in their room.

Telephones

Of course you are no stranger to the telephone, your link to "a life!" If possible you should talk your parent(s) into two ultimate communication features in order to ensure you never miss that "Come over. My parents are out of town." call. They are call waiting and ring master. These cost just a few dollars more a month and maybe you can offer to pay for them. Ring master allows you to give a number out to your friends and, when they call, the phone will ring a certain way. This way you can tell if the phone is for you or your parent(s). Call waiting makes sure you never miss a call by beeping if you are already on the line. This is a must for emergencies.

Closets

Always pick out what you are going to wear the night before and have it ironed and ready. Organize your closet. There are stores which have all sorts of efficient storage bins and racks for a closet in order to maximize space. Make sure you organize your closet before school starts.

Bedrooms

In order for your days to start off smoothly, make sure you get up at least one hour before you have to leave your house. If you ever find yourself with some extra time in the morning, great. Take advantage of this time and look over some notes from one of your morning classes. Remember, no matter what else you do in the morning, at least eat breakfast, and make your bed. So when you are gone all day, your parent(s) will only have wonderful thoughts about you when they look at your neatly made bed. As opposed to the thoughts they will have when they look at your unmade bed. Make sure you get at least eight hours of sleep a night and do not forget to set your alarm clock.

Environment

When organizing your own household environment, make sure you take care of the world's environment too. Get information on recycling programs and set up programs in your house. Tell your parents to buy only recycled paper products such as paper towels and toilet paper, and make sure to recycle everything that is recyclable. For help in setting up your home recycling program pick up a copy of *50 Simple Things Kids Can Do to Recycle* by the EarthWorks Group, 510-841-5866.

Now that you have organized your room and your house, you need to organize the most important aspect of high school, your classes.

Chapter 6

WHAT CLASSES SHOULD I TAKE?

There are many cool things about high school, but probably one of the coolest besides your new friends, your new parties and your new curfew, is you will actually be able to decide on what classes you want to take. No, this doesn't mean you can take five Music Appreciation classes and sit back and listen to Pearl Jam all day. What this means is, although certain classes must be taken to get through high school and into college, you now have some options to pursue subjects you enjoy.

When deciding on what classes to take, check with your academic advisor and your parent(s). The classes you completed in grade school will help determine what classes you need to take in high school. Some classes have "Prerequisites", that is other classes which must be taken before a particular class. For example, Algebra I must be taken before Algebra II.

It is important you and your academic advisor map out a four year plan. You want to plan your mandatory classes (ones you must take) and your electives(classes you get to pick), keeping an eye on your future plans for college and a career. I know it sounds like a lot to think about, but do not worry, that is why you have an advisor. You need to make sure you check with him or her at least two times a year, if not more. Your advisor will be able to tell you the classes you need each semester and each year in order to graduate from high school, prepare for your career goal and college admissions.

Most high schools hold a registration day or evening. Registration usually happens in the second semester/spring of 8th or 9th grade. Your class schedule, along with an information packet, usually comes in the mail before registration day. A week before school starts, they usually have orientation day. At this time, you can meet your teachers, see your classrooms, talk to other students, get your locker and generally check out your new high school campus.

Most high schools set up a meeting with you and your guidance counselor or academic advisor. This is the person(s) who will help you with your registration, scheduling and any questions you have about your new high school. Throughout the year, your advisor will set up meetings with you to see how things are going. This is the person to go to if you need help with any aspect of high school. If he/she cannot help you, you will be directed to a person who can.

My academic advisor/guidance counselor is_____.

His/her office hours are _____.

Rm #_____ Phone#:_____.

The most important thing to remember about your counselor/advisor is to use them to the maximum! If you have a question or a problem, go talk to them. Your academic advisor/counselor should be able to help you with the following:

1. new student orientation
2. academic problems
3. personal problems
4. courses to take each year
5. testing and test results
6. referral to counseling services
7. evaluations and recommendations
8. graduation requirements
9. selection of colleges and college preparation.
10. career awareness

Every high school is different when it comes to advisors/counselors. All counselors have a group of students who are assigned to them. Although they will have scheduled meetings with you, **it is your responsibility to make sure you check with your counselor/advisor at least once a semester.**

(You should check with them more often.) This is especially important when it comes time to sign up for classes. You want to make sure you take all of the classes necessary each semester to keep you on track for graduation.

As a freshman, however, most of your classes are mandatory. Your school registration packet should have a form very similar to the charts below. All high schools will give you a course handbook which contains information on required classes, charts to help you map out a four year schedule, credits and graduation requirements along with a description of each class. Your parents and advisor will help you understand this information and fill out the necessary forms.

Use the following charts to help map out your high school classes.

| Freshman year | | | |
| 1st semester | | 2nd semester | |
Classes	Credits	Classes	Credits
1.		1.	
2.		2.	
3.		3.	
4.		4.	
5.		5.	
6.		6.	
7.		7.	
8.		8.	
9.		9.	
10.		10.	
Total:		Total:	

Courses requiring approval/prerequisites:

Extracurricular activities and/or sports
I want to participate in:

AP (Advanced Placement)
Courses I might take:

Advisor's Signature:_____

Parent's Signature:_____

Sophmore year			
1st semester		**2nd semester**	
Classes	Credits	Classes	Credits
1.		1.	
2.		2.	
3.		3.	
4.		4.	
5.		5.	
6.		6.	
7.		7.	
8.		8.	
9.		9.	
10.		10.	
Total:		Total:	

Course requiring approval/prerequisites:

Extracurricular activities and/or sports
I want to participate in:

AP (Advanced Placement)
Courses I might take:

Advisor's Signature:_____

Parent's Signature:_____

Junior year 1st semester		2nd semester	
Classes	Credits	Classes	Credits
1.		1.	
2.		2.	
3.		3.	
4.		4.	
5.		5.	
6.		6.	
7.		7.	
8.		8.	
9.		9.	
10. Total:		10. Total:	

Course requiring approval/prerequisites:

Extracurricular activities and/or sports
I want to participate in:

AP (Advanced Placement)
Courses I might take:

Advisor's Signature:_____

Parent's Signature:_____

Senior year 1st semester		2nd semester	
Classes	Credits	Classes	Credits
1.		1.	
2.		2.	
3.		3.	
4.		4.	
5.		5.	
6.		6.	
7.		7.	
8.		8.	
9.		9.	
10. Total:		10. Total:	

Course requiring approval/prerequisites:

Extracurricular activities and/or sports
I want to participate in:

AP (Advanced Placement)
Courses I might take:

Advisor's Signature:_____

Parent's Signature:_____

Remember, it is not easy to change classes once you register. Schools must schedule space, books, and teachers, so really think about your registration. If you have to change a class, usually it can be changed if it is submitted two weeks before the first day of classes in any one semester or only after a week into classes. This way the school can see if it is possible due to classroom space, books, and teachers. Each high school has a different policy here, so check to see the policy before you register.

In grade school, middle school or junior high, they will make sure you have taken all the courses necessary for high school. Some of you will be at different levels in subjects such as English, math, science and language. If you have done very well in any of these subject areas, you should talk to your parents and teachers about Advanced Placement courses. Your teachers and parents will help you decide if you should be placed in honors or AP "Advanced Placement" courses. These are available for certain subjects (mathematics, sciences and foreign languages) and are determined by the classes you have previously taken, your scores on entrance exams or specific placement tests and your grades.

In high school, there are all kinds of exciting programs in which students can participate. Advanced Placement, Magnet Programs, Awareness Work-shops, International Studies, and International Baccalaureate Programs, Dual Enrollment are just a few. Ask your advisor to tell you about any special programs available. Most high schools also have exceptional student programs for the disabled, and the hearing or sight impaired. If you are interested in these programs, ask your advisor or check your high school catalog.

When selecting your classes, take the most challenging subjects you can. Do not take a course just because you heard it was easy. The harder you are on yourself now, the easier high school and college will be. Do not be scared to try something new!!

It is a good idea to first make a practice schedule and see if you will have time for all of your classes, outside of class study time, work and sports or student activities. Go over this with your parent(s) and advisor and check Chapter 8 on Scheduling. Also find out how much outside of classroom time is required to do well in each class. Simply ask your teachers at an open house or your first day of class. This will help you schedule your days.

During high school, depending on where you attend, you might have to take several standardized tests in addition to your regular classes. Tests such as the NEDT (National Educational Development Test), the ITBS (Iowa Test of Basic Skills), SAT (Stanford Achievement Test) are designed to make sure you are learning what you are supposed to be learning. Your teachers will tell you what to do to prepare for the tests.

So hey, if you are ready for your first day of high school, then let's go...

REGISTRATION NOTES

Chapter 7

YOUR FIRST DAY OF HIGH SCHOOL.

Finally it is here, your first day of high school! How do you feel?

❏ Excited ❏ Scared ❏ Sleepy ❏ Totally Freaked Out

❏ Happy ❏ Extremely mellow ❏ Bummed

Please fill in your own:_____

Your locker

One of your first stops will be your new locker. Some of you have had lockers before and others have not. Usually two students share a locker in high school, so you will meet your locker partner the first day. Your locker is important. It is where you will keep all of your books, supplies, lunch, and coat . It is also where you will post one copy of your class schedule along with a picture of your favorite hunk or hunkette.

It is important you are considerate to your locker partner. You will see each other several times a day, every school day. Discuss how you want to organize the locker and make sure to give each other equal space. When organizing your locker, try to set your books up so you can take them out according to which class you have next. The best way to do this is take books for several classes and this way you do not have to go back to your locker between classes. Typically, you only have five minutes between classes, so it gives you more time to get to and ready for your next class.

The most important thing to remember about your locker is the combination. You might say this is not difficult and, you are right, it is not; However your first days of high school can be very hectic and sometimes, yes, you can forget three simple numbers. Write down your locker combo and put it in your wallet or purse just in case. Also, do not give your locker combination to anyone else, unless you want to open it one day to find all of your books have mysteriously disappeared .

A good tip for memorizing your locker combination is to think about a sentence (or three words) that describes how you feel about beginning high school and assign a number to each word. For example, your combination is 30-24-10. So you could say "I 30-hate 24-school 10". Hopefully your code will be more like "School 30-is 24-cool 10".

YOUR LUNCH TIME

Although high school is more challenging than grade school, middle school or junior high, they still allow you to eat lunch. In high school, your lunches will be anywhere from 20 minutes to an hour. During lunch, try, to unwind a little. After you eat, take a walk, shoot some hoops, or rap with your friends. You will find you have time to look over notes and study if you want. Try to relax and have a good lunch every day, so you are fresh for your afternoon classes.

YOUR CLASSES

On your first day of high school, you will be going to your actual classes. You should have most of your books from registration. Be sure to bring a notebook to each of your classes. In each class, write down the following:

1. teacher's name.

2. their office/planning room number.

3. phone number.

4. hours they can be contacted.

5. Also write down any special supplies or items you will need for this class.

During your first class, the teacher might give you his or her "syllabus" for the semester. A syllabus is a schedule, listing material to be covered, test dates and assignments. Immediately rip this up and throw it back at the teacher. (Just kidding!). You will need this in order to help you make out your schedule (see Chapter 8 on Scheduling). And yes, believe it or not, you might even get homework your first day.

During your first classes, make an effort to meet at least two new people you do not know. Try to remember some trait about each person and repeat their names and the traits twice to yourself after you meet each. This will help you remember their names. This is not as difficult as you might think. Simply lean over to them and say, "Hello, my name is_____.

I thought I would introduce myself since we are going to be in the same class." It is really simple. Just don't do this while the teacher is talking.

YOUR TEACHERS

The average high school teacher is really no different than your grade or middle school teacher. They make you sit in their class for about an hour. They lecture you and show you problems on the board. They even give you homework, papers and tests. Usually they give you more homework, more papers and more tests than grade school, middle school or junior high teachers. Some of you may have developed a bad attitude about teachers. You feel they are out to get you, to test you, and to take all of your time away from the fun things in life. Well, the first thing you need to do is look at teachers differently. You see, in no time in your life are you going to be surrounded by so many people whose job it is to help you. The people who work at the burger joint are not there to really help you. The clerk at the clothing store is really not going to help make you a better person by selling you clothes. A teacher's whole purpose is to help you become a better, smarter person. I mean his/her entire job is to teach you things so you can get whatever you want out of life. Teachers are definitely on your side. They are there to help you accomplish your dreams. When you succeed, they have succeeded. Teachers love to be able to say, "Yeah, I taught _____(your name) who is now a _____ (your dream). So it is important that you start to think of teachers differently.

Learn to get the most out of your teachers and their classes.(See Chapter 11 on The Class) Get every piece of information out of them you can. Remember, teachers are people just like you. Don't talk when they are talking and be polite, just like you would want someone to be polite to you. Make them explain their homework assignments thoroughly and do not be afraid to ask them a million questions. Oh yes, and do your homework and study hard for their classes. The homework and studying are for your benefit, nobody else's!

If you are having a problem with a teacher, you should simply talk to them about it. If you feel talking to them will not help or you are nervous about it, check with your parents or counselor. They will help you with any situation with teachers.

YOUR MANNERS

Every high school has a set of rules students must follow. Usually these rules can be found in the high school handbook and are explained to you during orientation. Getting in trouble in high school is a big waste of time! The only thing it accomplishes is more school. The last thing you want to do is to stay after school. You have football practice, volleyball practice, the mall, biking, reading, and hanging out with your friends. You have had enough class time by 3:00. Why would you want more?

Remember, the easier you make it on your teachers, the easier they will make it on you. If you do get in trouble or get caught doing something you are not supposed to do, whatever you do, be honest. Nobody likes someone who is such a wimp that they try to lie to get out of trouble.

And now, a quick word on cheating, because that is all it deserves. Cheating is for losers! Every time you cheat, you are just making it that much harder to accomplish your dreams. If you ever find yourself in a position when you are not ready for a test or an assignment, talk to the teacher. They will help you be prepared for the next test or assignment. In addition, do not freak out about one or two bad grades. Everybody, including your teachers and parents, have received bad grades before. It does not matter what grades you get, just what you learn from the experience.

THINGS I NEED TO DO BEFORE MY FIRST DAY OF HIGH SCHOOL

THINGS I NEED TO DO BEFORE MY FIRST DAY OF HIGH SCHOOL (CONT.)

Believe it or not, your first day of high school will be over as fast as it began. Don't worry, you'll have plenty more days like it ahead of you. At the end of your first day, sit down and make a list of things you need to buy and things you need to accomplish. One of the first things you'll need to do is make your schedule. So let's check out High School Bound's Super Scheduling Method.

Chapter 8

SCHEDULING

As a new freshman, your daily schedule will be very busy. When registering for high school classes, sports, and other activities, your parents and high school advisor should help you. It is important to ask your counselor, teachers and coaches, how much time their classes and sports will require. Also, talk with your boss about your work schedule. See what hours or shifts are available.

In order to keep up with all of the school work and activities in high school (and have the most fun), it is important to make a daily, weekly and monthly schedule. If your high school is really cool, they will provide you with a customized notebook complete with a high school calendar and schedule. You already know how to organize your room and locker for high school, so let's talk about organizing your schedule. Here is the *HIGH SCHOOL BOUND SUPER SCHEDULING SYSTEM:*

YOU WILL NEED THE FOLLOWING ITEMS:

1. Daily assignment/activity notebook

2. A one-week calendar

3. Large monthly desktop or bulletin board calendar

1. DAILY ASSIGNMENT/ ACTIVITY NOTEBOOK

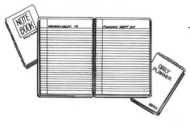

This notebook is carried with you daily.

REMEMBER TO:

1 Use to write down daily assignments in your classes and their instructions.

2 Use to write down specific daily activities you need to do.

3 Do your most difficult assignments first or study your most difficult subjects first.

4 Check items off when you have completed them.

5 Use study halls to the maximum. Try to get all of your work done during your school hours. (See Chapter 10 on Homework)

6 Always check the weekly and monthly calendar so you do not forget to correctly schedule your days.

Monday, September 19th

1 Spanish: read pages 15-25, do exercises 1,4,8. Learn new verbs!

3 Algebra: Do exercises 1-25, Chapter 3, Show all work

4 ~~Begin Studying for English Lit. Test, Review Chapters 1 & 2~~

2 Take Spike to the vet. Organize garbage cans for recycling

5

6

2. YOUR CLASS SCHEDULE.

Schools will provide you with a class schedule showing you the classes you are taking. Make (2) additional copies of your class schedule. Rewriting your schedule will help you remember it.

REMEMBER TO:

✔ Paste one in your locker

✔ Paste one in your assignment notebook or rewrite one there.

✔ Paste one on your bulletin board at home as part of your after school/ weekly schedule.

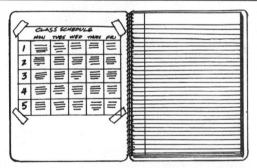
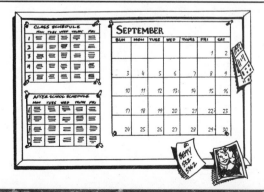

3. MAKE AFTER SCHOOL/WEEKLY SCHEDULE

This is a schedule for your activities outside of school time or after school.

Time	Monday	Tuesday	Wednesday	Thursday
8-3	Class Schedule			
3-4	Basketball Practice			
4-5				
5-6	Home Dinner	Home Dinner	Home Dinner	Home Dinner
6-7	Free Time	Free Time	Job	Free Time
7-8	Homework and Studying	Homework and Studying		Homework and Studying
8-9				
9-10	Free Time	Free Time	Free Time	Free Time
10-11	• Reading • Home Jobs • Hobbies	• Reading • Home Jobs • Hobbies	Homework and Studying	• Reading • Home Jobs • Hobbies
11-12	• Friends • Additional Study	• Friends • Additional Study		• Friends • Additional Study
12-7	Sleep			

REMEMBER TO:

Write in the time required for homework and studying. Try to study at the same time every night.

Write in the time needed for work and/or extracurricular activities.

Write in time needed for meals and sleep.

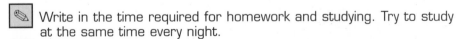

52

This schedule might change every few weeks. Simply write up a new one with your new activities and times. Also do not forget to check your monthly calendar at the beginning of each week for things which need to be done.

Friday	Time	Saturday	Sunday
Class Schedule	9-10	Free Time	Church
Homework and Studying	10-11	Job	Free Time
	11-12		Free Time
	12-1		Free Time
	1-2		
Dinner	2-3		Free Time
Free Time	3-4		
	4-5	Dinner	Dinner
	5-6	Free Time	Free Time
Basketball Game	6-7	Homework and Studying	Homework and Studying
	7-8		
	8-9		
Free Time	9-10	Free Time	Free Time
• Reading • Home Jobs • Hobbies	10-11	• Reading • Home Jobs • Hobbies	• Reading • Home Jobs • Hobbies
• Friends • Additional Study	11-12	• Friends • Additional Study	• Friends • Additional Study
Sleep	12-7	Sleep	

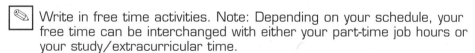

Write in free time activities. Note: Depending on your schedule, your free time can be interchanged with either your part-time job hours or your study/extracurricular time.

Paste up with your class schedule on your bulletin board and put one by the family phone so they know when/where you are for mesages.

4. Buy a large desktop\bulletin BOARD monthly calendar

Place in your home study area on a bulletin board or your desk.

Use to mark down long range assignments such as term papers, test dates, games, parties and the two R's "Rockers and Reviews".

Remember To:

 1 Write in test days.

 2 Write in long term assignment due dates and activities.

 3 Write in games, trips, and other activities.

 4 Write in the two R's:

Rockers = reminders of critical key exercises requiring study. "Rockers" are needed to rock your mind and remind you to do a particular task, such as history test in four days or English term paper due in three weeks. Always break large assignments up into smaller parts, such as when to have first draft done by, or 2nd book read by etc...

Reviews = are times needed for regularly reviewing all of your subjects. (Not just the night before a test either). This keeps the amount of studying constant. It also helps you avoid cramming for tests which can cause stress and other extremely uncool side effects like poor grades.

 5 Transfer important activities to your daily assignment notebook, For example: Begin reviewing for English Literature test or check out books for research paper.

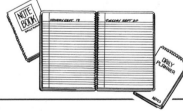

Monday	Tuesday	Wednesday	Thursday	Friday	Saturday	Sunday
1	2	3 Complete Outline for English paper	4	5	6 Pearl Jam Concert	7
8	9 Spanish Test Chps: 1-5	10	11	12 Basketball Game	13	14 Comlete 1st Draft of English paper
15 Monthly review in all classes	16	17 Job Training 7:30	18	19 Basketball Game	20 History test next week! Study this weekend	21 Volunteer Day "Pick up recycle"
22 Speech on "Pollution" Due	23 Complete final draft on English paper	24	25 History Test	26 Basketball Game	27	28
29	30 English paper due!!					

It is important to find out how much non-classroom time is necessary to do well in each class. Ask your teachers how much time is needed to do well in the class. The time varies from class to class, subject to subject. Keep in mind the average high school freshman does about **two hours of homework a night.** (O.K., please pick yourself up off the floor now.) Also talk to your coaches to see how long practice will be and do not forget the time needed to get to school and getting ready for school or practice. Remember, once you start school and all your extracurricular activities, you can adjust your schedule accordingly. Simply write up a new one which reflects the time you need to devote to each area of your life.

The previous pages are just sample schedules. Every student's will be different. It is important to use the High School Bound Super Scheduling format and tips. You do not have to schedule things in the exact time slots, but plan according to your preferences when you like to study or exercise or go to bed. If time allows, you might want to study after practice or after school, versus at night. Try to study at the same time every day. When scheduling your study time, do something physical with your study breaks. Take the dog for a walk, take the trash out, clean your room or even beat up your little brother or sister for a few minutes. (just kidding!).

If you are working part time, make your school schedule first, and then you will know what hours you are available to work. (See Chapter 13 on Work.) Unfortunately, most jobs give you the hours they need you, and not always the hours you want. Plan out your weeks and months carefully. Look at your work schedule keeping in mind upcoming test days. Try not to work a night before a test. However, if you schedule properly and stay up on all of your homework with regular reviews, working the night before a test will not be a problem. You can always speak to your boss and request certain hours, especially if you have worked at a job for a while. Making friends with your coworkers is also helpful, especially if you ever need someone to work for you.

Keep in mind you can create your own calendars or customize your own assignment notebooks. Use the samples in this chapter as a model. If you buy your own, remember, only buy those calendars and notebooks printed on recycled paper. They will be clearly marked with the recycled paper logo. Remember give your parents a copy of your schedule or show them where you hang yours. They will need to see it to plan their schedules.

PROCRASTINATION

Procrastination is the biggest enemy of almost every high school student. You know, putting things off until the last minute. Watching TV, shooting hoops or just cranking your stereo instead of starting your homework are all fine examples of procrastination. Here are a few pointers on how to combat procrastination (some tips are also listed in other chapters).

REMEMBER NOT TO BE L A Z Y!

Long term assignment should be started the day they are assigned. (Just a start will make the end seem attainable.)

If it is a reading assignment, begin to read the day it is assigned, even if it is just a few pages. If it is a paper, then quickly research the library for a topic which interests you or for any reference material you will need, and check them out.

Anytime you want to watch TV, ask yourself if there is any homework or long term project you could be working on now. If the answer is yes, then do not watch TV and start your project.

Zero homework rule. Do as little homework as possible by using your school time (study halls, time waiting for practice and lunch) to the maximum.

Yesterday's work should have been done yesterday. Try to complete all daily assignments the day they are assigned and not wait until the next morning. Start every morning with a clean slate.

When you feel like "blowing things off" and just hanging out, which occasionally is cool to do, remember one thing. If you regularly do just one thing for only a half an hour every day, you could accomplish some of the following things:

1/2 hour Activity	Daily Results	Yearly Results	Overall Results
Write books, letters, stories, diary entries	1 page	365 pages	Write 1 novel or 75 comic books or 24 short stories or enough letters to help poor people, neighborhoods, save the whales and trees, or any other charity you choose.
Worked job @ $5/hour	$2.50	$912.00	Major cash!!
Read books	8 pages	2,920 pages	Increase reading speed and comprehension, become smarter, read over 11 books. (250 pages each)
Help parents	1/2 hour	182 hours	Easily raise allowance and extend curfew!
Do sit ups and push ups	100 each	36,500 push ups 36,500 sit ups	Muscles and ripples!!
Go jogging & walking (1 mile in 15 minutes)	2 miles	730 miles	Healthy heart, lungs and happy dog!
Practice guitar, piano musical singing.	1/2 hour	182 hours	Learn to play instrument and several songs. MTV here I come!!
Pick up trash in neighborhood	30 pieces	10,950 pieces	Help the environment , make neighbors happy, make some $ recycling!

SCHEDULING A LOT

+ PROCRASTINATING A LITTLE

= A LOT DONE + THE MOST FUN

Chapter 9

STUDYING

Let's talk about studying for a minute. Tell me what you think about studying. I think studying is:

❑ **the worst possible torture**

❑ **the greatest joy in life**

❑ **a good way to spend a Friday night**

❑ **a great way to pass tests and keep teachers off my back**

❑ **the ultimate brain drain**

❑ **an intellectual stimulus**

❑ **too cool for comment**

❑ **the best way to reach my goals**

In Chapter 2 you thought about your study skills and determined which areas need improving. Although working to improve your study skills is hard, your improved study skills will make high school much easier.

TAKING NOTES:

Note taking is one of the most important, if not the most important study skill you need in order to succeed and survive in high school. Good notes from both your class lectures and your textbooks are necessary. Notes serve one main purpose, they help you remember what you have been taught or read, so take them!!

Good notes do this in three ways:

1st. Make you concentrate on the material being taught or read.

2nd. Make you go over material in your head.

3rd. Actually decrease the amount of material you have to study by providing you with a concise summary of all the important topics. This is particularly important around test time.

Too Much

In high school there is an easy, sure-fire method to make sure your note taking skills are good. If you are unsure about your note taking techniques, try the following. Take a minute or two after each of your classes or after school, and show each of your teachers your notes from that class. Ask them to review your notes to see if you have all of the important information. This should give you a variety of useful hints on how to improve your note taking skills. You can make this a lifelong habit, although it will not be necessary after awhile. Whenever you begin a new class, just ask the teacher to review your notes on the lecture. Doing this, just once, will give you some useful direction and feedback on your notes. Also, try to get to each class a minute early so you can get your notes ready and be prepared to *listen* right when the class begins.

Too Little

Here are the 9 notes on note taking:

1. Write down the main points of discussion and leave plenty of room between to fill in more detailed information.

2. Do not worry about writing down everything. The main points will allow you to reference your text book and fill in the blanks. However, **do not be afraid to ask teachers to slow down** if they are going too fast.

3. Make sure to **copy** all examples given by the teacher.

4. After class, **recopy** and **reorganize** your notes.

5. After the class or lecture, **recite** your notes.

6. **Review** previous class notes before new lectures. Review notes regularly.

7. Anytime you are assigned reading from a textbook, **take written notes.**

8. When taking notes from your textbooks, **read** a whole section before you start to take notes.

9. Write notes in your **own words.**

Too Weird

62

READING:

One of the major differences between grade school, middle school or junior high and high school is the amount of reading you will be assigned. The best thing you can do to improve your reading skills is to read. Over the summer try to read at least ten books, preferably more. Although most teachers would recommend reading literary masterpieces such as **The Grapes of Wrath** or **Animal Farm** and this is great advice, reading anything is better than nothing. Read a **"Skateboard Stunt Book"** book or **"Teens Guide to 90210"** or a book about a foreign country you have always wanted to visit. It is important to practice your reading.

In high school, you want to stay up on all of your reading assignments. Read a little bit every night. Start all reading assignments the day they are assigned.

Reading is more than just reading the words of any text. You can have your eyes on the page and your mind on tonight's game, last night's party or the babe or hunk sitting next to you. While reading general assignments in high school, you should use the SQ3R system developed by Frank Robinson at Ohio State University. **The SQ3R method is outlined here with a few additions:**

S=Survey: Skim over all headings, bold-faced sections, check out graphs and pictures and read questions at the end of the chapter. This will take only a few minutes and will give you an idea of what you are about to read and what you should learn.

Q=Question: Ask yourself "What am I suppose to learn in this chapter"?

R=Read: Read the material: First time without taking notes. Second time with taking notes.

   (See "Note Taking" above)

R=Recite: After reading the material and taking notes, try to recite what you learned.

R=Review: Review what you have read using your notes.

WRITING PAPERS:

In high school, you will be assigned many different papers to write. Some papers will be one page summaries, while others will be twenty page term papers requiring weeks of research on complex subjects.

There are different techniques for writing papers. Your high school teachers will probably give you some direction on how they want their papers written. Below are some basic techniques which will help you organize and write your high school papers.

1. Start them the day they are assigned.

The best way to avoid waiting until the last minute to start your paper is to force yourself to begin gathering your reference information or to read the assignment, the day the paper is assigned.

2. If allowed, always pick a subject which interests you.

Think about it. Would you be more excited about writing a paper on "The causes of the Industrial Revolution and its effect on modern agricultural economy" or "The cumulative effects of popcorn and Dr. Pepper on students at a horror movie?" The second choice definitely is more fun to research, however, you probably will not find it as a potential research paper topic choice. Most writing assignments give you a window of subject areas, and within those areas, you can pick a topic. Immediately check the library for topics which have plenty of information available and find one which interests you.

3. Research the right way.

First of all, learn how to use the library. Make a list of all possible information sources from books to magazines and write this list in correct bibliographic form. Your teacher will give you this form and do not forget to write down the library call number in case you have to find a book again. This will become your bibliography for your paper and writing it in correct form now will save you time later.

4. Get a three ring binder notebook designated for organizing and writing papers.

This "Paper Buster" will allow you to collect your research material and order it in any fashion you want. Make sure it has pockets to stuff in loose material until you punch holes in them. Organize your notes into a sequence and in a format which is easy to follow.

If possible, use a computer to write the paper. Use a wordprocessor with features such as spell checking and cutting and pasting. Store one copy of the paper on the harddrive and store one disk copy in your binder. If the computer is not yours, make two disk copies, one for the binder and one for anywhere else but the binder. You can print out hardcopies for storage and proofing whenever you feel it is necessary.

5. Research and collect information on your subject.

Gather and read all the material you will be using to write the paper. Some teachers want three different sources of information and others will not specify how many sources. Your library will have everything from encyclopedias and books to magazines on microfiche or CD-Rom which will be great sources of information . Your local or school librarian is also a good source of information. Talk to him or her about your topic and get ideas of where to find research material.

6. Make an outline.

Once you have researched your topic and organized your notes, make an outline. An outline should cover main topics and it will give you ideas to begin writing. This outline should follow an Introduction, Body and Conclusion format or whatever format your teacher assigned. Ask your teacher to review your outline so you do not waste time writing the paper incorrectly.

7. Write a first draft.

Do not worry about making the paper perfect now. Just try to write it. Fill in information under each of your outline headings.

8. Fill in and polish the paper.

Rewrite and rearrange (cut and paste) to further organize and complete the paper. Make sure the paper is organized and reads well, containing the introduction, body and conclusion. Double check for spelling and grammar.

9. Proofread the paper.

Have a parent, older brother sister, or friend proofread it. Make any changes or corrections necessary.

10. Spell Check one final time!

11. Print it.

Print the final copy and make back up copies (disk and hardcopy). Prepare to hand in either on time or even early!

REGULAR REVIEWING

The difference between an easy, fun, stress free, high school education, and a nightmare, marathon cramming session, is reviewing. Reviewing must become a routine. Even if you do not have homework in a particular class, review each day's class material, each night. Also, once every two weeks, simply set aside two or three hours and review previously covered material in all of your classes. Reread any notes, rework a few problems and go over any previously covered material. Reviewing does not have to be intense, simply enough to keep the material in your mind. By reviewing regularly, you will make your high school days, especially around test days, midterms and finals, much more enjoyable!

TESTS AND QUIZZES

Believe it or not, taking tests and quizzes in high school is easy. Preparing for them is difficult. The harder you prepare, the easier a test will be. Begin to prepare for every test at least one or two weeks before the test. When preparing for high school tests, in addition to your regular reviews, you should do the following:

✍ 1. **Review your textbook.**

✍ 2. **Review your notes from class.**

✍ 3. **Rework homework problems.**

✍ 4. **List the problems or ideas you do not understand, and one by one work them or reread them until you understand. Most teachers will ask a day or so before a test if there is anything you do not understand. By starting to study a week before, you will know if you have any questions.**

When studying for a test you can read things once, twice or even ten times. When preparing for a test you can work a math story problem as many times as you want, or until you get the right answer. Unfortunately when you are actually taking a test, you only get one shot at answering correctly. Take advantage of your study time before a test begins. Being prepared will also eliminate one of the biggest side effects of high school tests. Stress.

The best way to take any high school test or quiz is to be ready.

R=**Read** the instructions carefully. Ask the teacher if you have any questions about what you are supposed to do.

E=**Evaluate** the questions and time needed. Reread questions and be sure you understand exactly what is asked. Write down outlines for any essay questions and use process of elimination for multiple choice questions.

A=**Address** the questions you know. Answer as completely and as legibly as possible. If there is no penalty, guess on questions you do not know.

D=**Details:** Fill in additional details on your answers. Other questions on the test probably sparked your recall on some points you left out. If time allows review questions and fill in more detail.

Y=**Yo,** that was so easy, we did not even need "y".

If you run across any questions which are unclear, simply ask the teacher to clarify it. Do not try to guess at what is being asked. Be on the lookout for another problem, lack of time. Go into a test as prepared as possible and **follow the READY** guidelines. If the teacher allows you, ask for a little more time and if not, simply mark "time" on the questions you did not answer. If there is no penalty for guessing, any True/False or multiple choice should be answered and any essays should have an outline jotted down and marked "time."

What is the worst thing that could happen to you in high school? Waking up naked in the middle of the hallway? Getting caught skipping class? Or surprise quizzes? Certain high school teachers love to give surprise quizzes to make sure their students have been studying their material. The only way to counter this surprise attack is to be prepared. In high school, you should study for your classes as you would if you knew every teacher, in every class, is going to give you a pop quiz, everyday.

Whenever you get a test back, the teacher will usually review it during the class period. Reviewing tests and quizzes is important to help you learn what you missed. After you receive a test back, double check the grade to see why you missed what you missed. Be sure you hang on to all old tests for final review time.

GRADES:

I know a lot of you have been brought up to worry about grades. Well you know what, you should not worry about grades. Instead, worry about paying attention in all of your classes, doing your homework and studying everyday. If you do these things, your grades will be fine.

Whatever you do, don't let one bad test score get you down. If you do poorly on a test, do something you enjoy: go hiking, swimming, play one on one, call a friend, anything to renew your positive attitude. Then, as soon as you can, review your mistakes on the test, possibly with your teacher and get yourself back on track with the class. Getting a head start on the next exam's material is a good way to rebound from the depression of a bad score. (See Chapter 17 on Attitude)

This is an important section so I hope you paid attention, or even read it twice. Take some time now to make a list of additional books and activities to check out over the summer or in your spare time. Yeah I know what you're saying, "Like I don't have anything better to do?"

Make a very good list here.

1. *Read book on study skills*

2. *Take computer course*

3. *Read book on improving memory*

4.

5.

6.

7.

8.

9.

10.

11.

12.

13.

14.

15.

17.

18.

19.

20.

21.

22.

23.

24.

25.

26.

27.

28.

29.

30.

31.

Chapter 10

HOMEWORK

TELL ME HOW YOU FEEL ABOUT HOMEWORK:

❑ It is the greatest and I can not live without it.

❑ I hate it and I wish it were against the law.

❑ It is fun and I wish teachers would give me more.

❑ It doesn't matter because I never do it anyway.

Add your own:

Homework is defined as "work assigned during school hours that requires time outside of school or must be taken home to be completed."

There is one rule when it comes to high school homework. Try to do as little as possible. Yes, that's right, your mission is to do as little homework as possible and to leave all of your books at school at the end of each day. Now before you celebrate and rush this section over to your teachers and parents screaming no more homework, you had better read on.

THE WAY TO DO AS LITTLE HOMEWORK AS POSSIBLE IS TRY TO COMPLETE ALL OF YOUR ASSIGNMENTS AND STUDYING DURING SCHOOL HOURS. Although your high school day is filled with classes, you also might have 1 or 2 study halls a day. The best way to avoid a lot of homework is to use your study halls to the maximum and pay attention in your classes. Paying attention in class is another great way to keep homework to a minimum. If you really pay close attention to your class lectures, ask questions on topics you do not understand, and participate in classes you will not need to spend as much time after school studying. You have to be in study hall or school anyway, so why not use your time during school hours to get as much done as possible.

The first thing you need to do when assigned homework is to write the assignment down clearly with all directions. You can either do this in your notebook for the class or in a daily assignment notebook, which ever you prefer. Daily assignment notebooks have the advantage of keeping all your assignments in one place. This makes it easy to look at all of your homework at one time and to schedule. When assigned homework, try to look it over right away or before you leave for the day. If you have any immediate questions, you can ask the teacher who assigned it. This also allows you to estimate how long it will take to complete.

FIRST, COMPLETE THE HOMEWORK ASSIGNMENTS WHICH SEEM TO BE THE MOST DIFFICULT. This will allow you to work on the difficult material first when you are the most energetic and have the best concentration. Completing your most difficult homework while at school will allow you to track down a teacher or a friend if you have any questions. By using your study halls and free time during school hours, and by paying attention in your classes, you are able to leave many books at school instead of taking them home. In other words, you are doing as little homework as possible. Chances are you will still take a book or two home, but by using the time you are given during school

hours to complete assignments, you will have done as little homework as possible.

Now, for the homework you still can not finish at school, well forget about it........just kidding. Schedule a time each day after school or right after dinner where you do your homework. Try to do it at the same time each day. Most of you will probably have some type of practice or activity after school, so doing homework right after dinner is a good time. Try to study for an hour after dinner and take a 20 minute study break and then study one more hour. Make sure you have your own study area and study time set up at your house.(See Chapter 5: Organizing your room) If for some reason you manage to have a night with no homework, find a good book and read for at least 40 minutes. **It is important to have a routine of working your mind for a little bit every evening.**

ANOTHER GREAT THING ABOUT DOING AS MUCH HOMEWORK AS POSSIBLE WHILE IN SCHOOL IS, YOU DO NOT HAVE TO BATTLE THE MOST FEARED, DREADED, EVIL ENEMY OF HOMEWORK, THE TELEVISION SET. This 60 channel, sometimes more, cabled, high tech, colored monster, sits and waits for books to come home with weak little students and even try to be opened and read in its presence. With its far-reaching, control, it can capture unsuspecting students with homework to do and devour them for minutes, even hours!

DO I WATCH TOO MUCH TV?

Yes   No

❑   ❑   The first thing I do when I come home from any where is grab the remote control and turn on the TV.

❑   ❑   If I am not sure what I should do, I turn on the TV to decide.

❑   ❑   Even when I cannot find anything on TV to watch, I still flick through the channels several times to check.

❑   ❑   I dream about the characters on TV shows.

❑   ❑   I see my shoes, shirt, haircut, jewelry and favorite food on TV everyday.

❑   ❑   I watch shows again even though I have seen the episode before.

❑   ❑   I fight with other family members to watch what I want to watch.

❑   ❑   I watch MTV for more than 1 hour at a time.

❑   ❑   I have a TV in my bedroom.

❑   ❑   I watch at least three different TV shows a week.

ZONY TV

IF YOU ANSWERED YES TO **3** OR MORE OF THE ABOVE QUESTIONS, THEN YOU PROBABLY WATCH TOO MUCH TV.

❑   I watch too much T.V.   ❑   I do not watch too much T.V.

So every time you feel like picking up the remote control and plopping down on the couch for a marathon T.V. vegetation session, try reading instead. By reading more you will gradually be able to read and learn faster. Eventually, you will be able to read so fast, remembering all you have read and never miss your favorite TV shows.

ONE OTHER PROBLEM WITH HOMEWORK, BESIDES OF COURSE THAT IT IS A BIG DRAG, BORING, AND TAKES TIME AWAY FROM MTV, THE PHONE, HANGING OUT WITH FRIENDS, SPORTS, PARTIES, THE MALL, THE MOVIES AND ALL OF THE REALLY FUN THINGS IN LIFE, IS THAT YOU DO NOT ALWAYS KNOW ALL THE ANSWERS. Since you do not have a teacher right there to help, you might feel frustrated and want to give up. If, while doing homework, you ever come across something you do not understand or simply can not figure out, do not freak out. Mark the question, or problem or paragraph and go on. You can ask the teacher when you return to class the next day. Try to take a break from that particular problem or topic and study something else. Then go back to it and try solving the problem again. You might also try to see if an older brother or sister, friend, or even mom or dad can help. **Also remember to always read all of your instructions very clearly before beginning any assignments. Make this a life long habit to read everything before you start or sign it.**

While in high school, expect 2-3 hours of homework a night on average. However, you can complete a great deal of this in study halls or reduce the time it takes to complete by paying attention in class. You can finish the rest at home during the FTS or family study time.

Remember to follow the tips in Chapter 8 on Scheduling. Use your desk calendar to mark down long term homework assignments, like papers and tests. Write down "rockers" to remind you when to start studying for a test or whatever. Use your pocket notebook for daily and weekly assignments.

- **Footnote:** Note, it is o.k. to watch a little MTV and/or the Discovery Channel specials.

HOMEWORK ON HOMEWORK

1. What are two ways to do as little homework as possible?

2. What homework should you complete first?

    a. easy problems.

    b. any of your friend's homework, never your own.

    c. The most difficult assignments.

3. What is the most feared enemy of homework?

CHAPTER 11

CLASSROOMS, STUDY HALL, LIBRARY AND GYM

As a high school student, you are going to be spending a great deal of time in four different places. Classrooms, study halls, libraries and gymnasiums. It is important you know how to get the most out of your time spent in each of these places.

CLASSROOMS

So where is your favorite place on earth? The mall, the basketball court, your bedroom, the Grand Canyon, a R.E.M concert or _____(fill in your own). There is one more place you want to add to your list of favorite places, and it is the classroom. You must begin from this day forward to think of classrooms as places set up entirely to help you achieve whatever you want out of life. The chalkboard, the desks, the teacher, the whole room is only there because of you. Go into the classroom like you go into your other favorite spots, full of energy and ready to get as much out of it as you can!

Remember these 5P's and you will get the most out of your classrooms.

THE 5 P'S OF GETTING THE MOST OUT OF CLASS

1. PLACE YOURSELF

Where you sit in the classroom is very important. Studies have been completed on the relationship between where a student sits and his or her grades. If you want to get good grades in a class you should sit in the front row or toward the front in the middle. This position almost forces you to pay attention and limits the possibility of you falling asleep. The back and the sides are harder to pay attention with greater chances of talking to other students or becoming distracted. Sometimes teachers will simply place you in alphabetical order, and if this is the case make sure you follow the other 4P's.

2. PAY ATTENTION

In order to pay attention in the classroom, you have to pay attention to your eating, sleeping, and exercising habits outside of the classroom. Exercise regularly, especially if you are not playing a sport. Do not stay up too late watching MTV. Always try to have three good meals a day. Super Mega sugar sacks, pizza, and more pizza are not three good meals.

Even after taking care of yourself outside the classroom occasionally you will still find it difficult to pay attention. Maybe you like to daydream or just find the material boring. It is important to realize you have to learn the material sometime, so why not pay close attention now when you have to be in the classroom anyway. This saves you time at night from going over the material again and again because you did not listen to the teacher in class. One of the best ways to make sure you are listening and concentrating on the lectures is to follow number three and participate.

3. PARTICIPATE

Most students are not big participators. Some are shy, others don't know the answers, and some don't want to be defined by their peers (not real friends) as "brown nosers". If you have a question, ask it. The reason you are in the classroom is to learn. The reason the teacher is there, is to teach. Make them earn their money. Do not let them race through a lecture without explaining clearly, anything you do not understand. If there is something you do not understand, put your hand in the air and get the answer before you let the teacher move on. Do not let yourself fall behind in a lecture. The second you are lost, ask a question. Do not be afraid to ask any questions a lecture might prompt, even if it is not exactly on the subject; After all, the reason you are in high school is to learn. Also, do not read your text book or do your homework during lectures. The only thing you should be doing is taking notes on what is being taught today. (See Chapter 9 on Studying)

4. PERCEPTION

One of the biggest problems some students have with school is their erroneous (check the dictionary if you do not know what erroneous means) perception that a lot of the material taught will never be necessary in the real world. Well, you know what? High school is the real world! If you do well in high school, you can go on with your education and into any profession you desire.

5. PREPARE

Go to class prepared. Keep up on your reading. Do your homework. If you do not understand something, then go on to the next problem and ask teachers at the next class. Reread your notes to make sure you understand the material you have covered to date. If you go to every class prepared, you will never have to be worried about getting called on and not knowing the answer. If, by some remote chance, once or twice in your high school career, you are called on and do not know the answer, simply tell the teacher, "As a matter of fact, I was just about to ask you that very same question." The teacher will then have to answer it and you are off the hook.

In order for the 5P's to be effective, you must make sure you are in the classroom. Even high schools with Nazi storm troopers for hall monitors and Darth Vadar for disciplinarians, have ways that students can figure out to skip class. However getting caught is actually not the biggest problem with skipping class. Take a look at the "Blow Off Class vs. Go to Class" Comparison Chart:

"BLOW OFF CLASS   VS.   GO TO CLASS"

5 hours and = *Skip class 20 minutes	50 minutes = Attend class
• **50 minutes** Skipping Class (you're obviously doing something important during this time, right?)	• Take your own notes, get your own handouts.
• **60 minutes** Think of reason why you were not in class and prepare necessary forged absentee slips, catch school phone call to home and or prepare parent excuse and phony parent/teacher phone calls.	• Hear the lecture once. • Have opportunity to ask questions from the person who knows the answers.
• **30-40 minutes** Find someone, rap with them for awhile and borrow their notes & handouts.	• Avoid hassles and risk of getting caught.
• **25 minutes** Make copies of notes & handouts.	• Learn something and move closer to achieving your goals.
• **25 minutes** Return notes & handouts.	
• **45 minutes** Go over notes once since you did not hear lecture.	
• **45-60 minutes.** Could be longer. Figure out sections of notes, handouts or assignment you do not understand by asking friends or reading text.	

*Time frames given based on actual experience. Your mileage may vary.

In addition you run the risk of not understanding all the notes etc.. It will take five times as long to accomplish what one hour of class would definitely have accomplished had you attended. What you will definitely accomplish is the following:

Annoy friends who went to class by borrowing their notes.

Risk getting caught and spending more time after school along with parental harassment.

Run risk of inferior notes to the ones you could have taken.

Miss opportunity to ask questions from the only person who definitely knows the material.

STUDY HALLS

Study halls and the time you spend in them are extremely important. They are the greatest opportunity to accomplish one major goal of high school, which is, to do as little homework as possible. You have to be there anyway, so you might as well make the most out of it. Use your study halls to the maximum and try to get as much studying and work done as possible. Complete your hardest assignments first when your concentration is its best. This also allows you to track the teacher down for any questions while you are still on campus. If you find it difficult to concentrate and complete reading assignments during study hall, try doing your written assignments there. This will help keep your mind focused on your material.

LIBRARY

One thing you want to do before you leave middle school or junior high is learn the necessary survival skills to find your way around in a library. Do you think you have the survival skills to find your away around the endless towering forests of shelves and the sharp edges of the computerized catalog table? Or will you whimper in a corner unable to find a book, a newspaper, or even an article for you to munch on? Can you survive in a library? Well let's see!

EXPERT LIBRARY SURVIVAL TEST:

(Assume you are stranded in the library without a librarian to ask any questions.)

1. You have a one page paper due tomorrow on an article that was in Seventeen Magazine's 1994 January edition. You would find that by:

a) Calling any girl you know who is seventeen years old and asking her.

b) Check the Periodic Table of Elements under element Seventeen Magazine.

c) Check the card or computer catalog under title index Seventeen.

2. You need to find a book but you do not know the title of the book, only the author's name. You would

a) Check in the microfiche.

b) Check in the card or computer catalog under the author's last name.

c) Check all of the book shelves in an orderly fashion starting at the far left corner of the library.

3. You need to read an article that appeared in last Saturday's local paper but you did not remember to save the paper. You would

a) Check the microfiche.

b) Have the librarian announce over the loud speaker for any paperboys or papergirls to come to the front desk.

c) Check the library's newspaper section.

4. You need to see if the library has a book on the TV show Beverly Hills 90210. You would

a) Check by looking it up in the subject catalog.

b) Check in the media room .

c) Check in the U.S. Postal Index Directory of Zip Codes under 90210.

5. You need to write a paper on Ocean Pollution from only recent articles appearing in various newspapers and magazines. Your first step to find this information would be?

a) Check the subject catalog under Oceans.

b) Search either the printed or electronic index to periodical literature.

c) Call the Jacque Cousteau Society.

Correct answers can be found at the end of this chapter. If you missed any of the above you would not survive in a library by yourself.

SOME BASIC LIBRARY SURVIVAL TIPS ARE:

1. Libraries are usually arranged into several key areas:

Catalog area: You can find either computer catalogs, card catalogs or both, where you can look up books by author, subject or title. Your first stop for library survival.

Reference areas: You can find a variety of reference materials here. Dictionaries, yearbooks, encyclopedias and CD-ROM data bases, which give you access to all sorts of research material and indexes to magazines and newspapers.

Stack areas (Book shelves): You can find most of your books in these areas shelved by call numbers you get from the card catalogs.

Study areas: You can find booths, tables or rooms for quiet study.

Periodical areas: You can find current and back issues of magazines, journals and newspapers. Some are in print, some in microfiche or microfilm.

Media areas: You can find audiotapes, videotapes, diskettes, and other media, along with equipment to use them.

- Most libraries have both electronic catalogs and regular card catalogs to help you find material.

- The first place to begin to look for a book is in one of the catalogs (computer or cards)

- Materials in these catalogs are under either title, author or subject.

- Indexes help you find articles in newspapers and magazines.

- CD-ROM data bases accessible through computers may have everything from maps to magazines to books on them. Items can be looked up by just knowing a few key words of a topic or title. Also most libraries are wired into the Internet.

Spend some time in both your grade school library, your public libraries and your future high school library and make sure you can survive in a library!

GYMNASIUM

If you play a sport, you will already be spending time staying physically fit. If you do not play a sport, and especially if your work or hobbies do not involve exercise, it is extremely important to start a routine of exercising. Try walking, swimming, running, roller blading or aerobics. In addition, try lifting weights to increase your strength and endurance. If you need some ideas and even if you do not play a sport or are not currently enrolled in Physical Education, you can ask the high school PE teacher to give you a good work out program. By checking with a coach or PE instructor, you can get a brief lesson on exercises, proper stretching techniques and injury prevention. Make sure you have a complete physical before you start any exercise routine or sport. List some of the activities you plan on doing to stay fit:

Activity	Where	With whom	Days	Time

Exercise Routine: Circle Days: M T W Th F S Sun   Time:

Exercises	Repetitions/Time
1.	
2.	
3.	
4.	
5.	
6.	
7.	
8	
9	
10.	

LIBRARY SURVIVAL TEST ANSWERS:

1. c) Check the card or computer catalog under title index <u>Seventeen.</u>

2. b) Check in the card or computer catalog under the author's last name.

3. c) Check the library's newspaper section. (Note: It takes about a year to put papers on microfiche.)

4. a) Check by looking it up in the subject catalog.

5. b) Search either the printed or electronic index to periodical literature.

CHAPTER 12

HIGH SCHOOL SPORTS AND EXTRACURRICULAR ACTIVITIES

So, you are thinking to yourself one day you want to be a professional soccer player or a champion beach volleyball player. Maybe you want to be a world class ballet dancer or world famous rock star. Well, you know what? High school is the perfect place to begin to make dreams come true or at least have a ball trying! While in high school you should participate in at least one extracurricular activity. It does not matter what sport or activity you join, what is important is to pick one you like. Playing a sport is a great way to meet people, develop discipline, stay in shape and it can teach you teamwork. Participating in an extracurricular activity is a great way to meet people, develop discipline and learn skills which will help you in your future job.

SO WHAT HIGH SCHOOL SPORT ARE YOU INTERESTED IN:

❏ Baseball ❏ Basketball ❏ Dancing ❏ Fencing ❏ Football

❏ Gymnastics ❏ Handball ❏ Judo ❏ Karate ❏ Racquetball

❏ Soccer ❏ Softball ❏ Swimming ❏ Tennis ❏ Track and Field

❏ Wrestling ❏ Volleyball ❏ Other:_____

The coach is:_____

The sport starts:_____

I will need the following
equipment:_____.

_____

WHAT HIGH SCHOOL ACTIVITY OR CLUB ARE YOU INTERESTED IN:

❏ Band ❏ Debate/Speech ❏ Drama ❏ Environmental Work

❏ Journalism ❏ Politics ❏ Social Work ❏ Other:_____

The coach is:_____

The activity starts:_____

I will need the following equipment/supplies:_____

_____

_____

WHAT ARE YOU GOING TO DO TO GET READY FOR THIS SPORT OR ACTIVITY:

_____

_____

_____

Remember, you will be attending a school with many other students. Chances are you will no longer be the best basketball or volleyball player, the fastest sprinter in the school, or have the nicest singing voice. Also, without a doubt, you will no longer be the worst basketball player or volleyball player, slowest in the school, or have the worst singing voice. We already told you in Chapter 4 on Summer Activities that you should take advantage of your summer before freshman year. Well, we are going to tell you again. If you are interested in playing a sport in high school or participating in any extracurricular activities, there are three words to remember for the summer, **Practice, Practice and Practice!!** High school sports and activities are very competitive and although there will be a lot of students trying out for the teams, not everyone takes advantage of the summer to improve his/hers skills.

Certain high school sports start before the school year. Be sure to find out when try outs or the first day of practice is to be held. If you can make it on a team, great; if not, you should still play any sport you enjoy. Most high schools have very active intramural leagues. You can either work at your skills and practice for next season or you can find another sport or activity you enjoy. Some high schools have no cuts for teams freshman and sophomore years.

One of the best things about high school is the various sports, clubs, and organizations you can join. There are clubs to save the environment, clubs to work with handicapped kids, clubs to start your own business, you name it. Check to see the exact schedule for meetings or practices so you can schedule accordingly. Most activities are held right after school which makes it easy to schedule times and rides.

If you are going to participate in a sport or other activity you are going to be working with coaches or supervisors. It is important to remember most high school coaches are serious about their jobs. Do your best and be serious about the sport or the activity you are in. Put all your energy into every practice and always remember no matter how crazy the coach seems to be, you are doing this for the fun of it! High school coaches know school classes always come first and should work with you to make sure you are always putting your studies first. If you ever have a

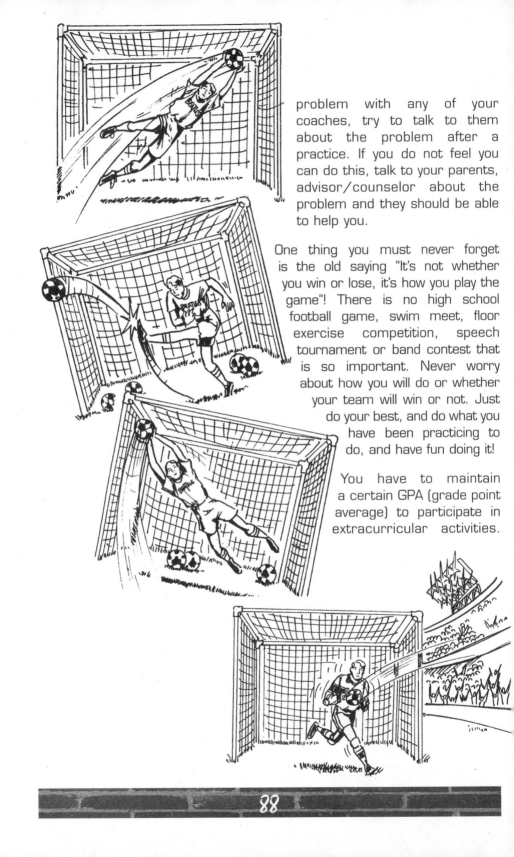

problem with any of your coaches, try to talk to them about the problem after a practice. If you do not feel you can do this, talk to your parents, advisor/counselor about the problem and they should be able to help you.

One thing you must never forget is the old saying "It's not whether you win or lose, it's how you play the game"! There is no high school football game, swim meet, floor exercise competition, speech tournament or band contest that is so important. Never worry about how you will do or whether your team will win or not. Just do your best, and do what you have been practicing to do, and have fun doing it!

You have to maintain a certain GPA (grade point average) to participate in extracurricular activities.

If you schedule properly, this should not be a problem. If you are having trouble keeping up with your school work and playing a sport or activity, then you should speak to your coach and counselor to determine a plan of action. Maybe you just need help with your scheduling or maybe you need to take some time off from the activity or sport.

What happens if you do not want to play a high school sport? Well, that is o.k. just make sure you do some form of exercise regularly. Playing any sport just for enjoyment is great, taking karate or dancing lessons, running with your dog or hiking are all good options.

THE PHYSICAL EXERCISE I WILL DO SEVERAL TIMES EVERY WEEK IS

1. Walk my dog

2. Go jogging

Chapter 13

Working

All of you are probably going to work at some point during high school. Working part time is great! There are many jobs where you can make money and learn some skills which will help you later. No matter what job you take, there is always something you can learn from it. Washing dishes can teach you about a kitchen or how a restaurant works. Washing cars can teach you about customer service and working as a team. Make sure you know your exact school schedule before you commit to a job. It is very important you schedule your school obligations first and then see how much time you have available for work.

A weekend job or one which requires only two nights a week would be good. It is extremely important that you explain to your boss you will put in honest hard work for him or her when you are working, but high school comes first and you will let him or her know in advance if there are conflicts. A special concert, student elections requiring some extra time, a sports tournament or any other school related activity are all important events and should be attended. Any boss who is cool will understand and work with you on scheduling.

Before you begin any new job it is very important to ask a few questions and make sure you fully understand all of the terms of your employment. You might have a tendency to avoid asking these important questions up front because you are so happy about getting the job or whatever, but it is good business practice. Any boss with half a brain or even a quarter of a brain will understand that these questions should be answered before a person begins work:

REMEMBER to ask

1. What are my exact responsibilities for the job? (known as Job Description)

2. What training will I receive for the job?

3. Do I get paid for training?

4. What are my hours and how and when do you schedule hours? (every 2 weeks, once a month)

5. How much do I get paid?

6. Does the company offer me any other benefits besides my normal pay? (Insurance, sick pay)

7. Who is my supervisor(s)?

8. What are the rules for sick days, vacation days and all employment policies? (What happens if I miss work etc....)

9. To whom do I talk if I have a problem with the job?

10. What other jobs or advancements could this job lead to?

11. Can they place my checks directly into my bank account?

✔ Get items 1, 3, 4, 5, 6, 8 in writing. Most companies will provide an employment packet which contains this information.

✔ Keep track of the hours you work in your own notebook in addition to your time card.

✔ Before you sign anything, review any forms requiring your signature with your parent(s).

THERE ARE A FEW PRACTICES WHICH YOU SHOULD FOLLOW AT EVERY JOB YOU EVER HAVE:

1. **Do your best at everything you do.**

   Whether it is washing dishes or cars, or cutting grass or hair, by doing your best you are starting a pattern of always doing quality work and are building a good list of recommendations and contacts.

2. **Get to every job a little early and stay until the end.**

   Being on time for work and always asking if there is anything else you can do right before you leave are great habits bosses and coworkers will always remember.

3. **Ask as many questions as possible about the job or business.**

You are there to make money, but get more than money out of any job you take. Learn as much as possible about the business.

4. **Treat everyone you work with fairly and honestly.**

It is important to treat everyone in this manner, but especially at work where you might need someone to cover for you one day if you are sick or have a test the next day.

5. **Whatever you do, always give a two week notice if you have to quit a job.**

There is an old saying which says, "Don't burn your bridges." This is extremely important advice. Throughout high school you will probably hold several jobs, some full time and some part time. Always leave employment on a good note so you will always have good references for future jobs.

6. Remember school is the priority now and it always comes first!!

WORK STUDY

Most schools have work study programs. Work study jobs are great! They make it easy to schedule around school activities and they are easy to organize transportation to and from work. Your high school packets will contain information on work study jobs available.

POTENTIAL PART TIME JOB CHART.

Employer Phone	Contact	Interview/ Fill out application	Pay Hours/ Days	Job Descript.	What I can learn
Burger King 361-6862	Mr. Chase 3:30	Monday May 1	$5/hr 3-9	cashier	cash machine, customer service, food purchasing

MONEY

In addition to learning a great deal while working at any job, there is also the benefit of being paid. Your first step in handling money is to get a job and make some. Your second step, which is actually just as important as the first, is learning how to keep it. Before you start high school, you need to open a savings account at a bank. Your parental figure can help you with this and hopefully at least provide you with enough to open the account. If not, find a bank that has a minimum amount to open an account, usually around $10.00. It is very easy to open an account. Just walk into a bank and ask to see someone about opening a savings account and they will sit down with you and explain how to open the account and how to make deposits and withdrawals. You will probably have two forms to sign and make sure you get a copy of everything and keep it in your personal file at home.

So you have your job, you have your savings account, now for the fun part. Let's think about something you want to buy. Let's say you like a new CD player or mountain bike. Maybe you need some new shoes or have found a sweater that you really like. Or hey, maybe you need next year's tuition. Let's take an example of something you would like or need, and see how much we need to save to reach your goal. Always remember these things when shopping for something you want:

SHOPPING TIPS

$ Check at least three (3) places for prices before buying. (The phone works nicely here.)

$ Research the brand you want to buy. Look at brochures from different brands to compare features, costs etc. More importantly, find a friend or relative that bought one, and talk to them.

$ Find out exactly where you would take your item (stereo, walkman, bike etc...) to be fixed if it breaks.

$ Make sure the product is returnable if you are not satisfied.

$ Save all receipts, tags and warranties that come with your product.

What I would like to save for or buy

How much it costs: $

Look at the chart below to see how much you would have to save and for how long, to come up with the money you need:

MONEY SAVINGS PLAN TO ACCOMPLISH GOAL:

If you save	3 mnths	6 mnths	1 yr	1.5 yrs	2 yrs	3 yrs	4 yrs	5 yrs	10 yrs
$5/week for	$65	131	267	407	552	854	1174	1515	3559
$10/week for	$130	263	535	815	1104	1708	2349	3030	7119
$15/week for	$196	395	803	1223	656	2562	3523	4595	10,679
$20/week for	$261	527	1071	1631	2208	3416	4698	6060	14239
$30/week for	$392	791	1606	2447	3312	5124	7047	9090	21358

WITH PARENTS MATCHING PROGRAM.

Parents Match per Week	3 mnths	6 mnths	1 yr	1.5 yrs	2 yrs	3 yrs	4 yrs	5 yrs	10 yrs
$5=$10 per week	$130	263	535	815	1104	1708	2349	3030	7119
$10=$20 per week	$261	527	1071	1631	2208	3416	4698	6060	14239
$15=$30 per week	$392	791	1606	2447	3312	5124	7047	9090	21358
$20=$40 per week	$523	1055	2142	3262	4417	6832	9397	12120	28478
$30=$60 per week	$785	1582	3213	4894	6625	10248	14095	18180	42717

(This assumes an annual interest rate of 6% and deposits made every week. Interest is the amount of money a bank pays you for letting them use your money.) Ask your banker to suggest options here.

You can see just saving a little money every week really adds up. In order to help you set up a matching program we have enclosed the **High School Bound Money Matching Contract.** Simply remove the contract and present it to whomever you think would want to match your contributions. This could be any parental figure, aunt, uncle, older brother or sister. Make sure you both read the contract carefully and sign it. Then all you have to do is start saving!!

HIGH SCHOOL MONEY MATCHING CONTRACT

This Contract is made between

_____and _____
<small>(Your name: herein referred to as Saver)</small>　　　　　<small>(Person(s) matching name: herein referred to as Matcher)</small>

RECITALS:

1. The "Saver" is trying to save money for various reasons and wants to open a savings account. The "Matcher" wants to help and assist the "Saver" to save money for various reasons by opening a savings account and matching the monthly deposits of the "Saver".

2. The "Saver" and the "Matcher" have set up a joint savings account for the sole purpose of starting to save money at the _____(name of bank). The bank Account number is_____.

3. "Saver" and "Matcher" agree to perform under the terms and conditions set forth in this contract. In consideration of the mutual promises set forth herein, it is mutually agreed as follows:

TERMS:

RESPONSIBILITIES OF "SAVER"

"Saver" will make the best effort to save money on a weekly basis and deposit this money into a savings account every week.

RESPONSIBILITIES OF "MATCHER"

"Matcher" will make the best effort to match the money deposited by the "Saver" on a weekly basis and deposit this money into the joint savings account every week.

MONTHLY DEPOSIT/MATCHING AMOUNT

The amount to be deposited by the "Saver" every month will start out at $_____ which is to be matched by the "Matcher" for a total monthly deposit of $_____. This amount can vary from month to month.

"SAVER" WITHDRAW OPTIONS

Check one:

_____"Saver" can withdraw money without permission of "Matcher" but must do so for responsible and necessary purchases or purposes only.

_____"Saver" can only withdraw money with permission of "Matcher". "Matcher" must not unreasonably withhold permission to withdraw, but must let "saver" make responsible decisions when taking out money.

DURATION & TERMINATION

The parties hereto contemplate this contract will run for 4 years from the date hereof and in the absence of written notification by either party of cancellation, this contract will run from year to year up to a maximum of 8 years.

Independence of this agreement from all other family matters

No family fights or disagreements can get in the way of this contract and must be treated separately! "Matcher" cannot withhold matching payments as punishment or even if there is currently a fight or problem in the house. "Saver" cannot withhold monthly savings deposit or act irresponsibly with money as punishment or even if there is currently a fight or problem in the house.

MONTHLY REPORTING

The "Saver" will be responsible to keep track of all monthly statements, deposit and withdrawal receipts and other paperwork.

The "Matcher" has total unlimited access to these records at anytime.

IF A MATCH PAYMENT IS MISSED

It is understood from time to time maybe a deposit will not be made or a match payment missed. It is a critical part of the agreement, that every month some amount, no matter how small, is deposited and matched. The contract is still good and enforceable if a payment is missed, and both the "Saver" and "Matcher" must simply make up the necessary amount on the next deposit.

This contract is written under the laws of the State of _____ with its parties residing at_____.
(Your address)

Agreed to this_____day of _____, 199____.

Signed by_____
(Saver) Student

Signed by_____
(Matcher)

Chapter 14

YOUR FAMILY

PARENT(S)

Let's talk about our parent(s) (Parents = a mom or a dad or an adult who is responsible for you. You know who I mean, the person or persons you are supposed to ask if it is o.k. for you to stay out until 11:00). Check off what you think about your parent(s):

MY PARENT(S)		
❏ are cool	❏ are strict	❏ understand me
❏ don't understand me	❏ are loonies	❏ are super loonies
❏ are super	❏ (add your own)_____	

The best way to get along with your parents is to make life easy on them by following a few simple rules, and perhaps some hard ones.

First of all, it is important that you get to know your parents. I know what you're saying, "Hey, I have lived with these people all my life or most of my life, I think I should know them by now." Well let's make sure you do. Make time now to sit down with your parent(s) and ask them a few questions. Here, I will get you started:

1. What was the funniest thing that happened to you in high school?

2. What are some of the things you wanted to do for a job when you were young? (Wanted to be an astronaut, a singer...)

3. What was your best subject? What was your worst subject?

Add your own questions for your parents here:

Hopefully, throughout your high school days you will never hesitate to ask your parent(s) questions about anything and you will let them ask you anything. I know some of you probably feel you want your parents to mind their own business and let you do whatever you want. You know what? Your parents would probably like that too.I mean come on, you are in high school now, you should have more independence! The best way to get more independence is through totally honest communication or **"T.H.C."**. If you involve your parent(s) regularly in what you did last night, what happened at school today and in general, give them regular doses of T.H.C., then they will feel informed and will give you more independence. The worst thing you can do to your high school independence, is to lie to your parents or not involve them in your activities.

Let your parents know about parent conferences and different ways for them to get involved with your high school. Coaching, volunteering and just plain giving you rides to events are all great ways for your parents to get involved.

So what happens if you are having trouble with your parent(s)?

If you and your parent(s) get in a fight, remember these three things:

1. T.H.C. (totally honest communication) This is always your first step. Talk calmly about whatever is bothering you or your parents. Have them say everything that is on their mind while you listen and then when they are done, you say everything that is on your mind.

2. Listen to what they are saying more than how they are saying it. Many times when parents are mad, they yell and say things that do not make sense. It is important to listen for the message first. Realize that if your parent(s) did not care about you, they would not even bother to discuss anything with you at all. Also, ask your parents to do the same.

3. Finish what you started. Always try to come to a mutual understanding about what the fight is all about. Do not just yell at each other. Before you

conclude your conversation try to have answers for, "How are we going to make sure this doesn't happen again?," and, "What did we both learn from it?"

One final note about your parent(s). Take advantage of every opportunity that comes up to thank them for what they do for you. Doing some extra things around the house, babysitting a time or two when you might not want to, or even just a thank you note, are all certain to lead to more independence and nicer parent(s). **Take time to make a list here of things you could do to make life easier on your parents and just possibly happier for you!**

1. Clean my room without being asked.
2. Ask them on a Saturday morning if there is anything they would like done.
3. Make dinner for them one night a week.
4.
5.
6.
7.
8.
9.
10.
11.

BROTHERS AND SISTERS

Whether you are a big brother, big sister, little brother or little sister, or an only child (apply these tips to friends), it is important to remember just two things in order to get along.

1. Your brothers and sister are just like you: they have dreams; they get mad; they are messy; they might like their own bedroom; they do not like taking tests; they like talking on the phone; they get worried about school; they have problems with their friends; all of these things and more, **just like you.**

2. Try to always put yourself in their place whenever there is a problem or fight. Whenever problems arise, the very <u>second</u> you feel there is a problem, immediately think how they might feel about the situation.

3. Make a list of things you could do to be nicer to your brothers and sisters and things they could do to be nicer to you. And, have them make their own lists.

WHAT I CAN DO TO BE NICER TO MY BROTHERS AND SISTERS:

1. Let my younger brothers or sisters know I can help them with homework.

2. Shorten my phone conversations or call friends back if my brother or sister really needs the phone.

3. Don't take so long in the bathroom in the morning.

4.

5.

6.

7.

8.

9.

10.

11.

WHAT MY BROTHERS AND SISTERS CAN DO TO BE NICER TO ME:

1. Always ask to borrow any clothes and hang them up when they are finished.

2. Keep their part of the bedroom cleaner.

3. Listen and talk to me if I have a problem I want to discuss.

4.

5.

6.

7.

8.

9.

10.

11.

Before you begin high school, make a list for each of your brothers and/or sisters. By communicating now about some ways to be nicer to each other, you should avoid some fights later on throughout your high school days.

PETS

Name them, feed them, water them, clean up after them, train them, play with them, take them to the vet for check ups.

WHAT DO YOU DO IF YOU HAVE PROBLEMS AT HOME AND YOU DO NOT THINK YOU CAN TALK TO YOUR FAMILY ABOUT THEM?

Unfortunately some of you might find yourself in a situation where you have a problem at home and you do not feel you can help by talking to your parents, parent, brothers or sisters. Maybe there are big fights, your parents hit you often or one of your parents is drinking too much. You feel you should not say anything to anybody. However, **if you feel you need to talk to someone, then you probably should.** If your parents or parent seem to be having a problem, maybe you and your brothers and sisters can work things out and speak to them together. If you do not want to talk to another family member or if you do not think it would help, then check with your school counselor. Counselors will listen and give advice on how and where to get help. It is very important to use your counselors at the high school, that is their job! Use them!

Chapter 15

MEETING PEOPLE, FRIENDS AND DATING

MEETING PEOPLE

I know that some of you are thinking, "What if I don't meet anybody in high school, and nobody talks to me or even knows who I am? What if I have no friends, no one to talk to or go out with on a Friday night? What then??" Most of you are worried about meeting people at your new school, but you really should not be. High school is not only a great place to meet people, it can be an easy place to meet people if you remember a few suggestions. Remember that every other freshman in your new class is also worried about meeting people.

The classroom is the first place where you will meet people. Really make an effort to meet at least two people your first day of class in each class. All you have to do is turn towards another person and introduce yourself. Yes, it is that simple! Everyone in the classroom is new to high school just like you. They are thinking about the same things. They are nervous about the same things and they will be happy to meet someone new, just like you will be. Extracurricular activities are another great place to meet other students. By becoming involved in at least one extracurricular activity you will meet new people who like some of the same things you do. Remember, although you want to be outgoing, when you first start hanging out with new people, always listen more than you talk. This way you can sort out the goons from the cool people.

WHEN MEETING PEOPLE FOR THE FIRST TIME REMEMBER:

- 😈 Be courteous. First impressions are very important.
- 😈 Listen carefully. It is important to show a sincere interest in what other people say.
- 😈 When told someone's name, repeat it either to yourself or out loud and memorize it.
- 😈 Don't judge a person by appearance.

In high school, not everyone you meet is going to be nice. Unfortunately, you will run across people who brag and make fun of other people. These people should be avoided. If they want to know why you don't go to parties with them or why you do not talk to them a lot, simply tell them you do not like how they treat people. Maybe they will start to be more considerate and you will eventually hang out together.

If you seem to meet people easier than a friend, always try to include your friend in your activities with new friends. Do not become a babysitter for your friend. Do what you would like them to do for you if you had trouble meeting people.

FRIENDS: GIRLFRIENDS AND BOYFRIENDS

Eventually you will find yourself hanging out with a certain group of people who have become your friends. Your group of friends might change sometimes, which is fine and normal. So how do you know who are your friends and who are not?

WHO ARE YOUR FRIENDS...	WHO ARE NOT YOUR FRIENDS...
•Those who are happy for your accomplishments.	•Those who are unhappy about your accomplishments.
•Those who encourage you to pursue whatever interests you.	•Those who discourage or make fun of you for pursuing whatever interests you.
•Those who always try to include you in their activities.	•Those who do not make an effort to include you in their activities.
•Those who say nice things about you behind your back.	
•Those who notice when you're depressed and try to cheer you up.	•Those who say mean things about you behind your back.
	•Those who never notice how you feel.
•Those who don't try and pressure you to do things you do not want to do.	•Those who try to pressure you to do things you do not want to.
•Those who always tell you the truth, even when it hurts.	•Those who lie to you.
•Those who are cool according to the cool vs uncool chart. [see page 113]	•Those who are uncool according to the cool vs uncool chart. [see page 113]

If you have someone you consider a friend but they do not treat you as one, talk to this person right away. Tell them what made you upset. Usually, if the person is really a friend, they will understand and work on being a better friend. Sometimes friends will say something which hurts you. Many times your friend is actually just trying to get your attention.

There is one golden rule if you always remember you will never go wrong when it comes to dealing with your friends. **"Always treat people just like you would want them to treat you"**.

WHAT SHOULD YOU DO WHEN YOU AND YOUR BOYFRIEND OR GIRLFRIEND GO TO DIFFERENT HIGH SCHOOLS?

Absolutely nothing. Do not worry about it. Both of you will meet many other people during your years in high school. The best thing you can do for yourself and your grade school sweetheart is:

1. Be honest with each other and try to stay in touch. You can still hang out with a person even if you don't attend the same high school. In fact, it is great because you can meet people from other schools.

2. Agree to see other people during high school. By agreeing to see other people, neither of you can cheat on the other. You are not saying you like each other any less. You are simply being mature about your separation.

3. Take great care of yourself by studying hard, participating in many activities, and striving to reach your goals.

WHAT HAPPENS IF YOU MEET SOMEONE WHO YOU REALLY LIKE IN HIGH SCHOOL BUT THEY DO NOT LIKE YOU?

Well, obviously you should fling yourself from the top of the school in protest. Actually, no, maybe you should throw them from the top of the school. **WRONG.......** Unfortunately, not everyone you want to date or "go out with" is going to feel the same way. This is perfectly normal and some couples are much better friends than they are boyfriend and girlfriend. If you like someone, but they only want to be friends, there are two things you should do.

1. Talk to a close friend about it. By talking about it you will get it off your chest and that automatically makes you feel better.

2. Follow number 3 above and take great care of yourself. By doing this, you will feel good about yourself and, by staying busy with activities, you will meet other people and chances are you'll find someone else you might like.

WHAT HAPPENS IF I WANT TO BREAK UP WITH MY BOYFRIEND OR GIRLFRIEND?

High school is a time of tremendous change. A person's goals change, as do their lifestyle and relationships. If you are with someone who is not giving you the consideration you feel you deserve then here are a few pointers on breaking up and moving on:

1. Do it honestly. You must talk to this person and tell him/her how you feel. Do not have someone else talk to them. This is your responsibility. There is no one way to tell another person you do not want to go out with them as boyfriend and girlfriend. Maybe go over what you want to say with a close friend and make sure to be completely honest and considerate of the other person's feelings.

2. Try to remain friends. Many times couples are better friends than they are boyfriend and girlfriend.

3. Do not let anyone make you feel guilty about the break up or harass you. If you were honest with the person, you have nothing to feel guilty about. Do not tolerate being harassed. You should talk to your friends and counselor if this occurs.

WHAT HAPPENS IF MY BOYFRIEND OR GIRLFRIEND WANTS TO BREAK UP WITH ME?

1. Unless you know you have been unfair to this person and have given them a reason, never take a break up personally. You obviously have a lot of great traits, which is why they wanted to be with you in the first place.

2. Talk to a close friend or friends about the break up. This always makes you feel better.

3. Whatever you do, do not just sit in your room and be depressed. Decide on being sad for one day, two at the most and then get busy! Take great care of yourself by studying hard, participating in many activities and striving to reach your goals. By doing this, you will feel good about yourself and, by staying busy with activities, you will meet other people and chances are you will find someone else you might like.

DATING

Once in high school all of you are going to be at one time or another faced with the opportunity to go on a "date". Now, I do not know if you are aware of this, but dates are not just a guy asking a girl out and they go to a movie or something. First of all, girls can and should ask guys out on dates if they want to. Secondly a date can be a group of people going out to the mall, a party or a football game. **Here are some Do's and Don'ts of Dating:**

Do's	Don'ts
Do always be courteous to your date even if you do not think you like the person.	**Don't** ever judge a person just by looks.
Do go on double dates or group dates on any first dates.	**Don't** drive up to a house and honk the horn to pick up a date.
Do let your parent(s) know exactly where you are going.	**Don't** do anything you don't want to just to impress your date.
Do bring your date home when you are supposed to.	**Don't** ever pressure someone to do something he/she does not want to do.
Do be on time to pick up a date or to be picked up.	**Don't** lie to get out of a date.
Do always tell the truth to people who ask you out.	**Don't** kiss and tell.
Do always walk your date to the door.	**Don't** forget to thank your date for a good time.

RESPONSIBILITY IN RELATIONSHIPS

Upon entering high school you will have many more freedoms and many more choices. Chances are very good several times during your high school years situations will come up where you have the opportunity to either make out or have sex with someone. There is nothing wrong with developing a close relationship with a boyfriend or girlfriend, but this does not mean you have to have sex with this person. In high school, you might feel pressure to go farther than you want to. Do not let yourself be talked into anything. If a person really likes you and cares about you, they will not pressure you to do things you do not want.

The best plan for avoiding any heartaches, sexually transmitted diseases (STDs) and any unwanted pregnancies is abstinence. If you don't have sex, you cannot get or get someone pregnant. This is an equal responsibility of both males and females. You and your boyfriend or girlfriend can still be very close without having sex. Talk about this subject with your boyfriend or girlfriend. Tell them exactly how you feel and listen to how they feel. You are older now and must take on some responsibilities. Responsibilities include abstinence and the obligations that go along with being intimate with another person. Don't worry. If your boyfriend or girlfriend truly cares about you, he/she will wait. They will still see you, still call you, and they will wait, because it is the best way!

It is important that you know everything there is to know, to prevent sexually transmitted diseases such as AIDS. Check with both your teachers and your parent(s) if you have any questions. Do not rely on another student, who by the way is probably trying to talk you into doing something you don't want to, for information on this topic.

GOSSIP, RUMORS AND THE TRUTH

Unfortunately, in high school students love to talk. The worst habit a person can get into is to gossip. It is not a good feeling to think other students are talking about you, especially if what they are saying is bad or untrue. A good rule to follow to avoid this trap is, *"UNLESS YOU SAW IT AND IT IS GOOD NEWS, DON'T TALK ABOUT IT."*

When dealing with anyone, from your friends and family to your teachers and bosses, always tell the truth. If you get in trouble in school or at your home, simply tell the truth. It is the only way the problem will get solved anyway. If you are in a situation where you really feel you can not tell the truth, talk to your counselor. Sometimes by going over a situation with someone who is not involved, makes it easier to figure out a solution. Start from your first day of high school to just plainly tell the truth in every case.

HIGH SCHOOL BULLIES AND BULLIETTES

One of the toughest, hardest working and most famous Presidents in the history of the United States who led this country through a Civil War and wrote such great speeches as the Emancipation Proclamation, once said, "It is not what you are called, it is what you answer to". Of course, this person was Abraham Lincoln. Unfortunately, just like in grade school, middle school or junior high, during some point in high school you are going to run across a bully or bulliette. This is a person who has to put other people down, call them names, or push them around.

Almost always, bullies and bulliettes are people with very low self esteem who need to insult others to get attention or make themselves feel better. Remember, bullies and bulliettes have the problem, you don't. The best thing to do when you run across these people is to ignore them. If they continue to bother you or your friends, then you must take a stand. This doesn't mean you have to launch an assault on someone. It means simply you must do something! Talking to a person one on one is the best! Tell the bully or bulliete that when they push people around, or insult people, it just makes them look stupid, that nobody in school likes it and, "If you have a problem with me, let's get it straight now and forget about it". Usually, unless they are real creeps, they will think about what you said and start to treat people better. If this still does not fix the situation, ask a teacher or counselor for some advice.

SO DO YOU WANT TO BE THE MOST POPULAR PERSON IN YOUR SCHOOL?

Well if you do, the first thing you must do is forget about trying to be popular. What you need to do is work on trying to be totally yourself. There is no one who can be a better you, than you. Remember being popular and being happy are not the same thing. The popular kids at schools have problems, things about themselves they do not like, and things they cannot do, just like you. If you want to be popular with everyone at school, try to be popular with just one person at a time. Be considerate to each person you talk to, be interested in what they say, and pretty soon, you will have a few good friends, and that is way cooler than being popular.

TO BE COOL OR NOT TO BE COOL, THAT IS THE QUESTION.

In high school everyone wants to listen to the coolest music, go to the coolest parties and hang out with the coolest crowd, right? Well, how do you know what is truly cool and what is not. Well just take a look at the "WHAT IS COOL AND WHAT IS NOT" CHART.

WHAT IS COOL	WHAT IS NOT
Studying and doing homework	Not studying and not doing homework
Paying attention in class	Talking in class
Asking questions in class	Making fun of people who ask questions
Really getting into a class you like	Just doing what it takes to get by in a class
Being supportive of your friends and encourage them with their interests	Making fun of your friends if they are doing something they enjoy just because you don't
Playing a sport	Playing dumb
Exercising	Not exercising
Joining the band	Talking about being a rock star without practicing
Reading all kinds of books	Not reading
Watching MTV or the Discovery channel	Watching TV all the time
Getting into hobbies: Cars, dancing, dog training	Getting into drugs: Alcohol, pot, cocaine
Part time jobs that are not too fun	Not getting a part time if you have the time
Clothes that are comfortable	Clothes that everyone else buys to try to be cool
Virginity	Sleazebagity
Being a peer pressure powerhouse	Being a peer pressure pushover
Judging people for who they are	Judging people for what they do or wear
Doing volunteer work with needy groups	Doing criminal work with greedy groups
Sticking by your friends when they need you	Not sticking by your friends when they need you
Being extremely popular with one good friend	Being extremely popular with a bunch of people who are not really your friends
Showing consideration for everyone you meet	Showing off
Trying to get along with everyone	Fighting
Saying words like "please," "thank you," "What can I do for you?"	Saying words like "Sh_t," "F_ _k," or "What can you do for me?"
Recycling	Littering

Remember, these days it is definitely way cool to be a good student. Today's nerds are tomorrows astronauts, MTV VJ's, doctors, missionaries, teachers, and marine biologists. Always strive to be and do your best at everything you do and strive and help others do the same. And have a lot of fun while you're at it!!

Chapter 16

PARTYING

In high school you are going to find yourself with more social opportunities than ever before. There will be parties every weekend. You will be meeting with your friends at the movies, the mall, football and basketball games, and the public library (where you always go to study, right!??) There is nothing wrong with partying. The truth is everyone from your high school principal and teachers, to your family and friends want you to have a great time in high school! However, nobody, from your high school principal and teachers, to your family and real friends, want you to do anything which might hurt you or others. Doing drugs is one thing that will definitely hurt you.

DRUGS

The most important thing to remember about drugs is to become educated and learn about them. Ask your teachers, counselors or parents whom you can talk to about problems with drugs and where you can get the right information. If your high school is cool, they will have a health class that teaches students about drugs and the hazards of trying drugs. Before you begin high school sit down with your parents and discuss drugs. Make sure your parents understand you want to be able to ask them questions or talk about drugs at anytime during your high school years. Never listen to the so called **DREKS ("drug expert kids")** who think they know everything about drugs and are trying to get you to try drugs. They obviously don't know the first thing about drugs or they would not be doing them. Remember there are some things in life which you can and should learn about without trying. Drugs such as pot and cocaine are illegal all the time. Alcohol will be illegal until you are 21 and then, only if you do not drive while drinking it. In addition to taking a class on drugs and any advice from parents, counselors and teachers, here are few things you need to remember:

CIGARETTES

GOOD	BAD
If you smoke next to someone you do not like, the smoke might bother them.	• Tighten blood vessels, make heart work harder. • Make it harder to breath by clogging small "cilia" or brooms which sweep out the dirt and unwanted particles from lungs. • Cause severe coughing. • Reduce your bloods ability to carry oxygen, thus effecting how your muscles and liver function. • Can be habit forming and addictive costing you hundreds of dollars each year. • Turn your teeth and fingers yellow. • Make your breath, hair, and clothes stink. • Can cause mouth cancer, lung cancer, gum disease, wrinkles, and heart attacks.

POT

GOOD	BAD
If you smoke pot you can get kicked out of school and you won't have to go to class anymore.	• Increased heart rate • Lack of concentration • Lack of comprehension • Paranoia • Similar effect on lungs as cigarettes • Jail and fines for illegal use.

COCAINE

GOOD	BAD
If you are caught doing cocaine you can end up in jail and that keeps prison guards employed.	• Ulcers in nose membranes • Increased blood pressure • Seizures • Death from cardiac arrest • Jail and fines for illegal use.

LSD, ANGEL DUST (HALLUCINOGENS)

GOOD	BAD
Using these drugs will keep drug dealers on the street then we can make TV police shows about them.	• Violent moods • Memory problems • Speech problems • Convulsions • Heart failure • Lung failure • Tremors • Loss of control • Depression • Insomnia • Jail and fines for illegal use.

ALCOHOL

GOOD	BAD
It is found in cough syrup and in addition, the purchase of large quantities of alcohol by you, can make a liquor store owner rich.	• Can cause liver damage. • Can cause kidney damage. • Can cause ulcers in your stomach. • Effects your coordination and thinking by slowing down nerve cells. • Can slow down your growth. • Can cause gastritis • Can cause ulcers • Can cause brain damage • Can cause pancreatitis • Can cause nausea and vomiting • Can cause cancer of esophagus • Can cause cirrhosis • Jail and fines for illegal use.

While in high school, whatever you do, always follow the
"3 NEVERS, NOT EVEN ONCE", RULES OF DRUGS.

1. NEVER GET IN A CAR WHEN YOU KNOW THE DRIVER HAS BEEN DRINKING OR TAKING DRUGS.

2. NEVER DRINK AND DRIVE.

3. NEVER TRY DRUGS LIKE POT, COCAINE OR CRACK, EVEN ONCE.

If, after reading about the harmful effects of drugs you still want to try them, just think about this before you make your decision. Think about where the drug you are about to try comes from, and what precautions have been taken to make sure it is safe for you to take. If the drugs are pot, cocaine or crack, you can be sure nothing has been done. Remember everybody's reaction to drugs is different. You never know how your body will react to a drug. One other thing to remember about drugs it is against the law. Getting caught the 1st time can mean 1 year in a correctional facility and/or fines up to $5000.

IF YOU HAVE ANY PARTICULAR QUESTIONS ABOUT DRUGS WRITE THEM DOWN NOW AND LATER ASK A COUNSELOR, TEACHER, OR PARENT.

If given a choice, most of us would choose not to try drugs, vandalize, or do things which might hurt ourselves or other people. Unfortunately, many times other people, even our friends, talk us into doing things we might otherwise not do. It is important you learn how to handle an everpresent dark force which lingers whenever and wherever high school students are gathered. This dark force is **"Peer Pressure"**. So, are you ready to stand up to this force? Let's see if you are a **"Peer Pressure Pushover" or a "Peer Pressure Powerhouse?"**

PEER PRESSURE TEST (circle the reponse you feel is appropriate) and be honest.

(1) Yes   (2) I might consider it   (3) No

1 2 3	If your friends wanted you to sneak out of your house after you were supposed to be in, would you?
1 2 3	If a group of other students were playing a beer drinking game at a party and asked you to join in, would you?
1 2 3	If one friend and you were alone and your friend wanted to drink some beer, would you?
1 2 3	If a group of friends wanted to vandalize a building and you were the only one who objected to doing it, would you still vandalize?
1 2 3	If some of your friends did not like a particular person whom you thought was nice and were not very nice to him, would you also treat the person rudely?
1 2 3	If you were on your first date with the person of your dreams who decided to try some pot with some people at a party, would you?
1 2 3	Just last weekend your close friends were talking about how they went farther than "making out" with their boyfriends and girlfriends. This weekend, would you try to go farther?
1 2 3	Next week a bunch of people are going to skip afternoon classes and hang out. They want you to go. Would you?
1 2 3	A bunch of your friends need a ride to a party and you are three months away from getting your driver's license. Your parents will be out of town that weekend and they are all begging you to drive to the party. Would you?
1 2 3	You have a big algebra test on Friday and one of your friends has stolen a copy of the test and has invited you over to look at it. Would you go over and study it so you know you can get a good grade on the test.

Now add up your score and circle it on the PPP scale to find out if you are a "pushover' or "powerhouse"!

_____ Peer Pressure Pushover	_____ Peer Pressure Powerhouse
1 2 3 4 5 6 7 8 9 10 11 12 13 14 15 16 17 18 19 20 21 22 23 24 25 26 27 28 29 30	

So how do you get the power to say no to drugs and fight the battle of peer pressure? Remembering the **4 C's**, and using them, that is how!

1. BE CONFIDENT:
How do you become confident? By trying your hardest at whatever you do. If you are into sports, then practice hard in any sports you play. Getting into your studies increases your confidence. By doing well in your classes, you will feel more confident in yourself and more relaxed outside the classroom.

If you have a hobby, really get into it. If you do not, then find a hobby that interests you and try it out. If you are into building things or sewing, then make your own little shop or sewing area in your basement, bedroom, or garage. Check out a book a month on your hobby from your library and read everything possible on it. Becoming an expert in your own hobby gives you confidence in yourself.

By developing confidence in yourself, saying no to any drugs or peer pressure situations is easy. You will feel you can look anyone straight in the eyes and simply say, "No." You can even say, "No thank you," if you want to be polite.

2. BE CAREFUL:
Be careful to learn all the facts about drugs, sex and the consequences of breaking the law. Whatever you do, do not rely on someone offering you drugs or trying to pressure you into some activity to tell you the truth about what is going on. Learning the truth about drugs and how they damage your body is the best way to help you say no to drugs. Learning the facts about sex and responsibility in relationships is the best way for you to be prepared to deal with those situations when they come up.

Be careful to think about the consequences of any of your activities also. Think about how you can hurt yourself, your friends, and your parents by doing drugs. Think about the consequences of becoming pregnant or getting a disease.

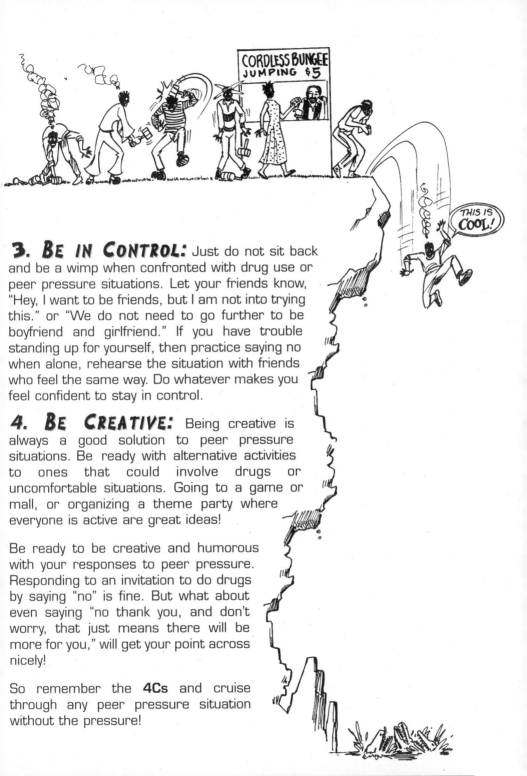

3. BE IN CONTROL: Just do not sit back and be a wimp when confronted with drug use or peer pressure situations. Let your friends know, "Hey, I want to be friends, but I am not into trying this." or "We do not need to go further to be boyfriend and girlfriend." If you have trouble standing up for yourself, then practice saying no when alone, rehearse the situation with friends who feel the same way. Do whatever makes you feel confident to stay in control.

4. BE CREATIVE: Being creative is always a good solution to peer pressure situations. Be ready with alternative activities to ones that could involve drugs or uncomfortable situations. Going to a game or mall, or organizing a theme party where everyone is active are great ideas!

Be ready to be creative and humorous with your responses to peer pressure. Responding to an invitation to do drugs by saying "no" is fine. But what about even saying "no thank you, and don't worry, that just means there will be more for you," will get your point across nicely!

So remember the **4Cs** and cruise through any peer pressure situation without the pressure!

Chapter 17

ATTITUDE

I know most of you would like to think high school is going to be one fun exciting day after another. It will be a great place to go where you hang out with your friends, get A's on every test, make every team you try out for, and have a great time at every party. However, this is not always the case. In high school you are going to be challenged with many new relationships, new classes and unfortunately new problems, both with school and your family. Here are some things that can cause you to be bummed out, stressed, depressed, or have a bad attitude:

☹ Getting a "D" on a test

☹ Getting in a fight with a friend

☹ Having a bad hair day

☹ Thinking you are too skinny or too fat

☹ Missing your favorite T.V. show

☹ Getting in trouble at work

☹ A friend not calling you to go out

☹ Your dream date not falling head over heels for you

☹ Your little brother breaking your stereo

☹ Your parents giving you a lecture

☹ Not having the money to buy something you want

☹   Add your own:_____

☹   _____

☹   _____

I THINK THAT MAYBE WE SHOULD SEE OTHER PEOPLE. SUE?... SUE?!?

OH GREAT A ZIT!

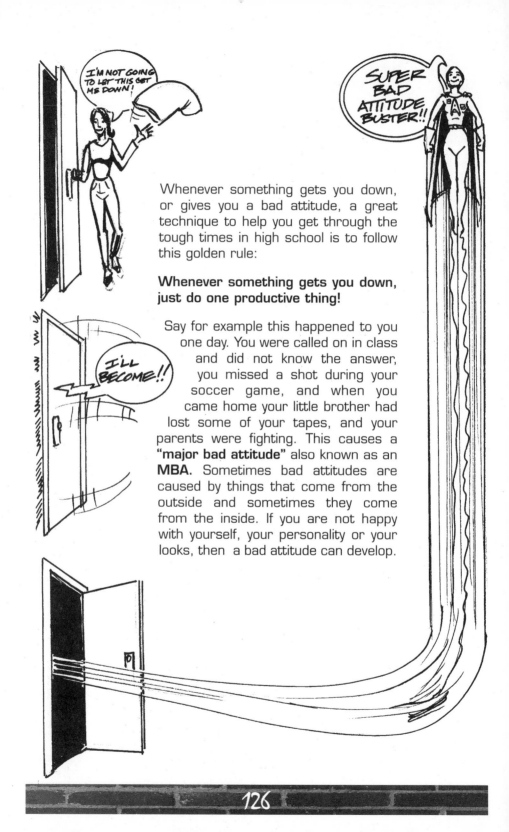

Whenever something gets you down, or gives you a bad attitude, a great technique to help you get through the tough times in high school is to follow this golden rule:

Whenever something gets you down, just do one productive thing!

Say for example this happened to you one day. You were called on in class and did not know the answer, you missed a shot during your soccer game, and when you came home your little brother had lost some of your tapes, and your parents were fighting. This causes a **"major bad attitude"** also known as an **MBA**. Sometimes bad attitudes are caused by things that come from the outside and sometimes they come from the inside. If you are not happy with yourself, your personality or your looks, then a bad attitude can develop.

SUPER BAD ATTITUDE BUSTER!!

I'M NOT GOING TO LET THIS GET ME DOWN!

So what should you do to make sure you do not let a bad attitude take over? **Well here are just few of the thousands of "productive things you can do to get out of a bad attitude":**

☺ Go for a walk or jog with your walkman and your dog.

☺ Do something nice for someone.

☺ Clean your room.

☺ Study an extra hour in your least favorite subject.

☺ Do an aerobics class.

☺ Review notes in one of your classes.

☺ Buy a book just for pleasure reading.

☺ Offer to run any errands for your parent(s).

☺ Call someone you have not talked to for a while.

☺ Read ahead in one of your classes.

I'LL BECOME!!

Add some of your own:_____

_____

_____

It is not so important what you do, just that you do something "productive" right away when you have a bad attitude! This is a great habit to get into for the rest of your life.

Whenever something bums you out or gets you down or makes you mad, just begin to do one productive thing, and watch how quickly your bad attitude will start to change.

Take a look at a few "MBA causers" and write down "one productive thing" you could do to help you handle them.

Attitude downers:	One productive thing I could do:
Getting a "D" on a test	
Getting in a fight with a friend	
Having a bad hair day	
Thinking you are too skinny or too fat	
Missing the TV show Martin	
Getting in trouble at work	
A friend not calling you to go out	
Your dream date not falling head over heels for you	
Your little brother breaking your stereo	
Your parents giving you a lecture	
Not having the money to buy something you want	
Have a big test you have to take	
Have to go to a party with a bunch of people you do not know	
Have to go to a meeting with a bunch of grown ups	
Have to give a speech in front of the entire class tomorrow	
Being sick and missing school, games and parties	
Your own:	

One way to help you maintain a great attitude throughout high school and your life is to occasionally take a spiritual break. This could be a nice relaxing camping trip or trip to a museum, regular Sunday visits to your church, or a hike through a park. If your high school offers a retreat program take full advantage of it. Retreats are where you and a bunch of other students take off for the weekend to a nice spot and think about the things that are really important in life. Take one per year if possible. A great spiritual break could also be doing some volunteer work at a youth center, hospice for the elderly, homeless center, or a community environmental group that picks up litter. Try to devote at least one morning or just a few hours at least once a month to some needy organization.

I think I would like to do volunteer work at_____.

If you decide that you need help with your attitude or any other area of your life such as communications, temper, self esteem, problems with your family, whatever, you should always remember to talk with your counselors. Talking with someone helps tremendously! Do not ever hesitate to talk to your high school counselor if you have a problem that you can not talk about with your parents, big brothers, sisters, or friends. They can offer advice or a suggestion of who could help you. It is important never to wait too long to talk about your problems with someone.

Chapter 18

CAREERS AND COLLEGES

I know you are thinking "Hey, I just finished reading about how to handle high school, why do I need to start thinking about college or my career already?"

It is never too soon to check out "what you want to be when you grow up". Summer is a great time to learn about any field or profession which interests you. Check out books and computer programs at the library about your potential profession. There are books available on every job from being a veterinarian and politician to an actress or nurse. Try to make your own field trips to any job which interests you. Ask your parents to take you to work with them for a day. If any of their friends are in a profession that you are interested in, see if you can go to work with them for the day.

So what do you want to be when you grow up?

- ❏ Astronaut
- ❏ Attorney
- ❏ Actress or Actor
- ❏ Boat Salesman
- ❏ Boxer
- ❏ Bartender
- ❏ CAT Operator
- ❏ Comedian
- ❏ Carpenter
- ❏ Doctor
- ❏ Dentist
- ❏ Deep Sea Diver
- ❏ Electrical Engineer
- ❏ Editor Sports Illustrator
- ❏ Editor Vogue
- ❏ Farmer
- ❏ Flight Instructor
- ❏ Freight Train Operator
- ❏ Grave Digger
- ❏ Goat Herder
- ❏ Gunsmith
- ❏ High Wire Artist
- ❏ Hang Gliding Instructor
- ❏ Horticulturalist
- ❏ Ice Cream Vender
- ❏ Illustrator
- ❏ Infantry Soldier
- ❏ Janitor

- ❏ Jockey
- ❏ Jazz Dancer
- ❏ Karate Expert
- ❏ Kindergarten Teacher
- ❏ Kennel Owner
- ❏ Language Interpreter
- ❏ Lawn Service Owner
- ❏ Legislator
- ❏ Model
- ❏ Mechanic
- ❏ Magician
- ❏ Navy Seal
- ❏ Naturalist
- ❏ Nothing
- ❏ Oprah Winfrey Guest
- ❏ Oceanographer
- ❏ Opera Singer
- ❏ Pet Store Owner
- ❏ Pianist
- ❏ Pharmacist
- ❏ Quality Control Specialist
- ❏ Quantum Leaper
- ❏ Queen
- ❏ Radio DJ
- ❏ Rancher
- ❏ Rock -n- Roll Singer

- ❏ Skateboard Shop Owner
- ❏ Scientist
- ❏ Ski Instructor
- ❏ Travel Agent
- ❏ Television Executive
- ❏ Transcriber
- ❏ University Professor
- ❏ Umpire
- ❏ Underwater Welder
- ❏ Volleyball Coach
- ❏ Velociraptor Researcher
- ❏ Veterinarian
- ❏ Weatherperson
- ❏ Wilderness Guide
- ❏ Windsurfer Renter
- ❏ X-Ray Specialist
- ❏ X-Ray Machine Maker
- ❏ X-Ray Machine Supplies Salesperson
- ❏ Yacht Captain
- ❏ Yak Breeder
- ❏ Yo MTV Raps Guest VJ
- ❏ Zebra Rancher
- ❏ Zombie
- ❏ Zoo Curator

POTENTIAL PROFESSION CHART:

What do I want to be when I grow up	What I am going to do to learn about this job.
Marine Biologist	*Go to work with parents, go to library and read about it, request a career week at your school, go to local aquarium and talk to biologist.*
MTV VJ	*Check out library for books. Call MTV see what information is available. Ask counselor about TV host careers.*

One very important habit to start is whatever job you do, whether it's babysitting, cutting grass, washing dishes, working at a yogurt shop or a movie theater, ask as many questions as possible. Learn as much about the whole business and not just your particular job. Ask where they get their supplies from or where is the best place to fix broken mowers and why. Ask how many bags of popcorn they need to sell per movie to make money or how many times they need to show a film to break even. A cool boss will appreciate your interest and will tell you as much as he or she can.

One of the first and best step to the profession of your choice is the college of your choice. Most high schools will introduce you to their college counseling office your 2nd or 3rd year in high school. Learn about all the resources available through your college/career counseling office. Talk to your counselors and parents about what high school activities you should participate in to prepare you for college and a career. Counseling offices have computer programs, videos, magazines and books which assist you in getting ready for and selecting a college and career.

Once in high school have an **ACADEMIC CHECK UP** every year to make sure you are taking all of the right classes necessary for high school graduation and college admissions. Your counselor or academic advisors will help you here. You do not want to end up your senior year in high

school not being able to graduate with your friends because you forgot to take one class. Think about having to stay in grade school another year, not a fun thought.

REMEMBER COLLEGE ADMISSIONS LOOK AT FIVE FACTORS WHEN DECIDING ON LETTING YOU IN OR NOT:

1. How hard were the classes you took in high school?

2. Rank in class/Grade Point Average.

3. SAT-I or ACT test scores.

4. Counselor/teacher recommendations.

5. Activities in and out of school.

6. Essay if required.

The best way you can prepare for college is to begin from your first day of high school and do the following:

- 📖 Do your best in all of your classes.

- – This will help your class rank and SAT-I or ACT scores.

- 📖 Participate in at least one extracurricular activity.

- – College admission offices love to see a student involved in other activities besides school.

- 📖 Use your academic advisor or counselor to the maximum.

> – Visit your advisor regularly and use all of your high school's resources to help you choose a college. This really becomes important starting your junior year.

• Follow the advice in this book.

– Learn good study and scheduling habits. Stay organized and stay busy. Do the best you can in your classes, your activities and your job. Be cool to your friends and family.

When the time comes get a copy of <u>How to get into and graduate from college in 4 years with good grades, a useful major, a lot of knowledge, a little debt, great friends, happy parents, maximum party attendance, minimal weight gain, decent habits, fewer hassles, a career goal and a super attitude, all while remaining extremely cool!</u> by guess who, Martin J. Spethman, and follow the advice found there.

THINGS I CAN DO NOW TO GET READY FOR COLLEGE AND A CAREER.

1. *Find out what college prep programs my high school offers.*

2. *Learn about career day or internships.*

3.

4.

5.

6.

7.

8.

9.

10.

Chapter 19

JUST FOR PARENTS:

This section is specially designed for parents of future high schoolers. It is packed full of helpful tips and organizational charts to help you get ready for you and your teen's next four years. So read on...

First of all, be proud of your offspring for having read or for reading *HIGH SCHOOL BOUND.*

You might tell them so.

We don't need to tell you everything you need to know about being a parent of a high school freshman. We want to provide you with a few good pointers about making the transition along with your child from grade school, middle school or junior high to high school. It is not important you remember and implement everything you read in this chapter. Even if you only remember one or two of the pointers here, you will have made your child's (and yours) hectic high school days more manageable.

Realize 8th or 9th grade is a time of tremendous change for kids. Understand they might seem slightly rebellious. Try to focus all of this energy into healthy educational activities. Whether your child attends public or private school, it is important that you take an energetic interest in your child's education. As a parent, it is wise if you make sure potential high schools are researched and visited. It is your responsibility to acquire and properly fill out all applications, financial aid forms or registration materials. It is smart to visit with other parents who have children attending your prospective high school. Make sure you participate in any orientation activities, talking to teachers and coaches. Of course, it is up to you to make sure all of the financial obligations from tuition to soccer shoes are addressed. Some of your children will be attending a public school based on where you live. It is still important to "check the school out" before your child attends.

Have your 8th and 9th graders learned everything they need to be successful in high school? As a parent, you should meet with your children's grade or middle school teachers in the fall of their 8th or 9th grade and see if they think your child is prepared for high school. If not, what activities can you begin now to help get them prepared. Talk to high school freshman counselors and teachers about what skills are important for high school and make sure your child is ready. To assist you with this area, here is a **LEARNING PROGRESS CHART** and **PERSONAL PROGRESS CHART** (student versions in Chapter 2) which you and your future high schooler should go over.

Let's see what areas they might need to improve. Here are a few question which will help you think about your child's study skills:

Yes	No	STUDY SKILLS
❏	❏	Can he/she read quickly and remember what he/she has read?
❏	❏	Can he/she write and spell correctly. Grammar and composition?
❏	❏	Can he/she write a speech, term paper and book review?
❏	❏	Can he/she add, subtract, divide and multiply. Can he/she do math story problems?
❏	❏	Does he/she have a solid base of knowledge in social studies?
❏	❏	Does he/she have a solid base of knowledge in sciences?
❏	❏	Can he/she use a computer?
❏	❏	Does he/she know how to use a library to get research material?
❏	❏	Does he/she know how to take notes for a class?
❏	❏	Does he/she know how to take notes from textbooks?
❏	❏	Is he/she good at scheduling activities?
❏	❏	Are his/her study skills good?
❏	❏	Does he/she like school and going to classes?
❏	❏	Are he/she good at organizing and keeping track of homework?
❏	❏	Does he/she get extremely nervous before tests?
❏	❏	Does he/she have trouble concentrating on school?
❏	❏	Does he/she daydream in class?

Now let's fill out your child's chart. Make sure you discuss it with him/her and the teachers. Ask your child the skills or subjects he/she thinks need improvement.

LEARNING PROGRESS CHART

Area or Subject that needs improvement	What will I do to assist my child in improving (Be specific)
Reading, he/she reads too slowly.	Encourge him/her to read 4 books a month and take a reading course..
He/she takes inadequate notes in class.	Talk to teachers after a few classes about reviewing my child's notes and check on how they could be improved.

Now, being ready for high school does not just mean your child is ready with good study skills. Is your child ready with personal living skills for high school?

Let's see what areas you think he/she might want to improve. Here are a few questions which will help you think about your child's personal living skills:

Yes	No	Personal Living Skills
❏	❏	Can he/she talk to you about anything?
❏	❏	Does he/she feel confident in their abilities to do new things?
❏	❏	Is he/she happy with their personality?
❏	❏	Is he/she happy with how they look?
❏	❏	Are there things about your child that they would like to change?
❏	❏	When someone makes your child mad does he/she handle it maturely?
❏	❏	Does he/she treat others like he/she would want to be treated.
❏	❏	Is he/she always honest with people?
❏	❏	Does he/she listen considerately to others?
❏	❏	Does his/her family talk to each other about problems?
❏	❏	Do you think there is something bothering your child that he/she has not told anyone about?
❏	❏	Does he/she usually look for negative things in people?
❏	❏	Does he/she worry about a lot of things?
❏	❏	Does he/she enjoy being by themselves on occasion?
❏	❏	Does he/she exercise regularly?
❏	❏	Is he/she happy with the way their friends treat them?
❏	❏	Is he/she always depressed?
❏	❏	Does he/she know the facts about drugs such as pot and cocaine?
❏	❏	Does he/she know the facts about sex?
❏	❏	Can he/she handle peer pressure and always make his/her own decisions?

Now let's fill out your child's chart. Make sure you discuss it with him/her and his/her teachers. Ask them the areas where he/she need improvement. After you have discussed this chart with your child, sign off on it.

PERSONAL PROGRESS CHART

Area or topic that needs improvement	What will I do to help my child improve himself/herself (Be specific)
Do not feel confident to do new things.	Take up challenging hobby or something you would really like him/her to do and practice. Maybe dance or karate lessons.
I am not sure that he/she really know about drugs.	Ask the counselor at school to give him/her information, ask teacher to have a drug class. Talk to him/her about having a discussion about drugs, not a lecture, and what he/she should know.

Make sure you fill out the charts with your 8th or 9th grader and begin any steps to improve his/her skills today!

WHAT ABOUT ALL THESE TESTS?

During 8th or 9th grade, there are several tests which may be given to see if students have learned what they are supposed to have learned up to this point in their schooling. The teachers (grade school and high school) can tell you what tests are administered by their school. The required tests vary from state to state and from private to public schools.

In addition to the above tests, which are for measuring achievement, most private schools have placement or admission exams. Preview or practice tests can be taken while in 6th and 7th grade. Scores from these admission or placement tests are usually interchangeable if students change their mind over the summer as to what school to attend. Public schools do not have admission tests; however, they do have standardized achievement tests in the fall after students get in. During your child's first year in high school, depending on where they attend, they might have to take several standardized tests in addition to their regular classes. Tests such as the NEDT (National Educational Development Test) or the ITBS (Iowa Test of Basic Skills) are designed to make sure they are learning what they are supposed to be learning.

Here is a chart where you can schedule any tests required of your child. You can find out which test needs to be taken by asking your child's teacher and by calling his/her future high school.

TESTS MY CHILD NEEDS TO TAKE FOR HIGH SCHOOL

TEST	DATE	TIME	PLACE

The best way to help your teens prepare for these tests is to make sure they are doing well with their regular school work. Here is a chart to help you plan any additional study activities.

Tests	Preparation Activities

SO WHERE DO I WANT TO SEND MY CHILDREN TO HIGH SCHOOL?

Information on any high school you want can be found by contacting them and asking them to send you their catalog and registration material. When you request information from a high school you should receive a packet with information on the tuition and fees, scholarships and work study, teachers, graduation requirements, grading system, rules and regulations, calendar, extra-curricular activities, honors, accelerated study programs and other basic information.

While researching high schools, talk to other parents, teachers, coaches and counselors. Make sure you attend any open houses and have your child spend a day at the high school he or she is interested in attending. Usually the "Open Houses" are held in the Fall for 8th & 9th graders. High schools also will come to your grade school or junior high and talk about their schools.

These are great opportunities to talk to teachers, coaches, and current students. Let's list the people you need to talk to:

PEOPLE	PHONE:
❏ Other Parents	
❏ Current students of potential high school	
❏ Spoke to Advisors/Counselors/Admission Directors	
❏ Teachers	
❏ Coaches	

HERE IS A CHART TO HELP YOU COMPARISON SHOP FOR A HIGH SCHOOL:

HIGH SCHOOL CHOICES	Name of school	Name of school	Name of school
❏ Acquired information on them. ❏ Acquired application forms.			
❏ High schools open house: Date: Time:			
❏ Spoke to people about school.			
❏ Other Parents ❏ Other Students ❏ Coaches			
❏ Counselors ❏ My teen			
❏ Comments			

HIGH SCHOOL CHOICES	Name of school	Name of school	Name of school
❏ Acquired information on them. ❏ Acquired application forms.			
❏ High schools open house: Date: Time:			
❏ Spoke to people about school.			
❏ Other Parents ❏ Other Students ❏ Coaches			
❏ Counselors ❏ My teen			
❏ Comments			

HIGH SCHOOL CHOICES	Name of school	Name of school	Name of school
❏ Acquired information on them. ❏ Acquired application forms.			
❏ High schools open house: Date: Time:			
❏ Spoke to people about school.			
❏ Other Parents ❏ Other Students ❏ Coaches			
❏ Counselors ❏ My teen			
❏ Comments			

It is important that you discuss any decisions with your child and include him/her in the process of selecting a high school!

SO HOW ARE YOU GOING TO PAY FOR IT?

If you are sending your kids to public school, you will not have to worry about tuition. However there are still plenty of fees, dues, supplies, books and personal items like clothes to consider. It is important that you check into all potential scholarships and sources for financial aid. When looking for financial aid you should check with your child's grade school, the high school he/she want to attend, as well as any local community groups. Financial aid can come in several forms for private schools.

$ Work Study based on need as part of a financial aid package. (Students work on campus)

$ Financial aid based on need.

$ School Academic scholarships based on grades and entrance exams given by high school.

$ Individual scholarships based on need decided by scholarship committee.

$ Community Academic scholarships based on grades and entrance exams given by some community group.

Here is a chart so you can keep track of your financial aid research.

POTENTIAL FINANCIAL AID OR LOANS

Bank or Organization					
Repayment terms & interest					
Forms/ information required					
$ amount					
Deadline					

POTENTIAL SCHOLARSHIPS

School or Organization					
Qualifications					
$ Amount					
Renewal Requirements					
Application Deadline					
Forms/ Information Required					

WHAT ABOUT ALL THE PAPERWORK AND REGISTRATION MATERIALS?

Dates and requirements for high school registrations can be found in the catalog or information packet. Once again these can be requested by calling the high school. Your high school registration packet will contain all or some of the following materials:

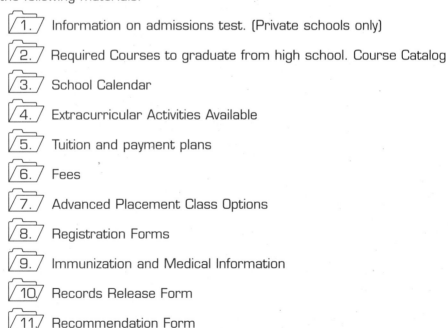

1. Information on admissions test. (Private schools only)

2. Required Courses to graduate from high school. Course Catalog

3. School Calendar

4. Extracurricular Activities Available

5. Tuition and payment plans

6. Fees

7. Advanced Placement Class Options

8. Registration Forms

9. Immunization and Medical Information

10. Records Release Form

11. Recommendation Form

You will need to fill out all forms and make sure you fill out any financial aid applications. Be sure to submit all forms before their deadlines and remember grade schools will send your child's grades to any high school you choose. Remember to take your future high schooler in for a complete physical and make sure they have recent immunizations. High schools will require proof of these. Also don't forget to make a copy of everything you submit.

SO WHO IS YOUR CHILD'S HIGH SCHOOL COUNSELOR OR ACADEMIC ADVISOR AND WHAT DO THEY DO?

Most high schools assign an Academic Advisor or Guidance Counselor to your child. This is the person(s) who will help them with their registration, scheduling, yearly academic check ups, academic and personal problems, and any general questions. Throughout the year this advisor will set up meetings with your child to see how things are going. This is who he/she can go to if he/she needs help with any aspect of high school. If the counselor cannot help, he/she will direct your child to the person who can.

My child's academic advisor/guidance counselor is_____.

Their office hours are _____.

Rm #_____ Phone#:_____.

Make an appointment with your child's counselor or advisor and jointly plan out your child's four year class schedule. Talk to your child's advisor at least twice a year. Let you are interested and you follow the progress of your child. The most important thing to remember about the counselor/advisor is to **USE HIM/HER TO THE MAXIMUM.** If you have a question or a problem, call them. Your teen's academic advisor/counselor should be able to help with the following:

1. new student orientation

2. academic problems

3. personal problems

4. courses to take each year

5. testing and test results

6. referral to other counseling services

7. evaluations and recommendations

8. graduation requirements

9. selection of colleges and college preparation.

10. career awareness

Every high school is different when it comes to the organization of the guidance office. Usually all counselors have a group of students who are assigned to them. Although they will have scheduled meetings with your child, it is your child's responsibility to make sure they check with their counselor/advisor at least once a semester. (You should check with them more) This is especially important when it comes time to sign up for classes. Your child will want to make sure they are taking all of the classes necessary each semester to keep them on track to graduate.

SO WHAT CLASSES WILL MY SON OR DAUGHTER BE TAKING?

The courses your child takes will depend on what he/she has taken in grade school, middle school or junior high and whether he/she has taken and scored well on any placement tests. Most of the freshman courses are mandatory. You will need to sit down with your new high schooler and discuss classes and help him/her map out a four year schedule. Your child's counselor will of course do this with them but it is important you review the selections. Your high school registration packet should have a form very similar to the chart below. All high schools will give you a course handbook which contains information on required classes, charts to help you map out a four year schedule, credits, and graduation requirements along with descriptions of each class.

In grade school, middle school, or junior high, your child should have taken all the courses necessary for high school. Students will be at different levels in subjects such as English, math, science and language. If your child has done very well in any of these subject areas then you should talk to their advisor about AP "Advanced Placement" courses. These are available for certain subjects (mathematics, sciences and foreign languages) and are determined by the classes your child has previously taken, their scores on entrance exams or specific placement tests and their grades.

In high school there are all kinds of exciting programs in which students can participate. Advanced Placement, Magnet Programs, Awareness Workshops, International Studies, International Baccalaureate Programs and Dual Enrollment are just a few. Ask your child's advisor to tell you about any special programs available. Most high schools also have exceptional student programs such as disabled, hearing or sight impaired programs. If you are interested in these programs, ask your child's advisor or check your high school catalog.

When reviewing course selections with your high school freshman, encourage him/her to take the most challenging subjects possible. The harder they are on themselves now, the easier school will become later. Always encourage your children to take on challenging subjects, activities, and jobs.

A chart to map out your child's course selection is found on page 35. Make sure you go over this chart with your child or use the one in the actual registration packet.

Map out a 4 year course schedule for your student. (See chapter 6)

Ninth Grade			
1st semester		2nd semester	
Classes	Credits	Classes	Credits
1.		1.	
2.		2.	
3.		3.	
4.		4.	
5.		5.	
6.		6.	
7.		7.	
8.		8.	
9.		9.	
10.		10.	
Totals:_____		Totals:_____	
Courses requiring approval/prerequisites:			
Extracurricular activities and/or sports I want to participate in:			
AP Courses I might take:			
Advisor's Signature: _____ Parent's Signature: _____			

Remember, it is not easy to change classes once you register. Schools must schedule space, books, and teachers, so really devote some thought to your child's registration. If you have to change classes after initially registering, it can be difficult. Usually schools can only make changes if they are submitted two weeks before the first day of classes or sometimes only after classes have begun. This is the only way schools can see if there is enough space, teachers, and books.

It is a good idea to first make a tentative schedule and see if your teen will have time for all of the classes, outside of class study time, work, sports and student activities. Go over this with your child and his/her advisor. Chapter 8 on Scheduling gives your child some pointers on making a schedule.

IN WHICH EXTRACURRICULAR ACTIVITY SHOULD MY SON OR DAUGHTER PARTICIPATE ?

First of all give your teen a great summer. Probably at this point your child already has a sport or hobby he/she enjoys. If he/she plans on participating in a high school sport, encourage him/her to practice, practice, and practice. Don't force your sons or daughters to participate in a particular activity just because you did. Look very seriously at all high school activities such as band, debate, or drama. All of these will instill great habits and teach useful skills to your teen, as you well know. Remember, the decision is ultimately your childs.

I THINK MY SON OR DAUGHTER SHOULD PARTICIPATE

in_____ and _____.

How do I organize the household for high school?

The logistical demands of having children in high school can rival a military operation on the scale of Operation Desert Storm. In order to meet the demands high school will bring

to your household, you must stay or-ganized and insist on cooperation.

1. Help Organize your new high schooler's room.

Whether your child has his or her own room, you need to guide him/her in preparing it for the new academic and social demands of high school. A high school student's room is important. He/she needs a place where he/she can read and study privately, as well as talk to friends and "crank tunes." Other members of the house-hold should know this and knock before entering the room. It is important they have a place to study and organize their school materials. For example, it could be a corner of the bedroom where you set up a desk and put up a bulletin board. In addition, if your teen's room has a window, invest in a high tech security camera to monitor it at night. Not for people trying to sneak in, but for people trying to sneak out!!

JUST FOR PARENTS

YOUR HIGH SCHOOLER WILL NEED THE FOLLOWING:

1. Desk or table with comfortable chair, a study area

2. Big wall/desk calendar to help keep track of activities and homework. (see Chapter 8 on Scheduling)

3. Notebooks, pens

4. Files or paper holder

5. Calculator

6. Dictionary

7. Atlas

8. Back pack

9. Alarm clock

10. Computer (Optional)

YOU WILL NEED A FEW ITEMS ALSO:

1. Wall calendar.

2. Daily planner

3.

4.

5.

6.

ADD YOUR OWN HERE:

**Make sure you schedule some time the afternoon or evening after your teen's first day of high school so you can go shopping for any supplies or items which are needed.

2. ORGANIZE YOUR KITCHEN:

A good investment for the kitchen of a family with high schoolers is plenty of tupperware. Your high schooler will have a new, busy schedule now. Practices, activities, and yes, even staying after school for disciplinary reasons, will all lead to a varied dinner schedule. If you do not do so already, plan out your meals at least a week in advance and make things that are healthy and can be reheated easily. Also shop for meals that your high schooler can make. And then obviously, you must show him/her how. If your family is small, plan dinner around the pratices. It's worth the inconvenience!

THINGS I NEED TO DO TO ORGANIZE THE KITCHEN	
Notepad on refrigerator door near the phone	

3. ORGANIZE YOUR COMMUNICATIONS

One of the most important things you as a parent can do to prepare your house hold for a high schooler is to open all lines of communications. Let your high schooler know that at any time, he/she can come to you with any questions or problems he/she is having. This is known as **totally honest communication or "T.H.C.".** You <u>must</u> establish T.H.C. before you and your teen embark on your high school adventure together.

At the beginning of the year, it is also good to let your future high schoolers know about the new rules. They will need more freedom now because they are in high school. But you must also tell them that you will need a few things. So make some rules that will make your life and your high schooler's life much easier.

RULES WE NEED TO HELP THE HOUSE FOR HIGH SCHOOL
1. Kitchen rules: who does the dishes, takes out the trash ?
2. Curfews: calling home when plans change....
3. Jobs around the house: walking the dog, cutting the grass...
4. Family study time hours (see below)...
5. Everyone makes his own lunches the night before...
Fill in your own

If you have not done so already, setting up a *"FBB" OR FAMILY BULLETIN BOARD* is a must. Your kitchen can serve as a great Command Center. Place your FBB by the home answering machine and make sure there is a note pad and pens handy. This will serve as a place to leave notes, lists of phone numbers of necessary people at school, emergency numbers, petty cash, calendars, and schedules such as the bus line, carpooling, or each of your children's practice schedules.

TELEPHONES

The most important thing when it comes to having high schoolers and phones in the same place, is to set up your phone features so your emergency calls are not missed because of your teen's emergency calls. Make sure you have **CALL WAITING** and if you have several teens in the house, **RING MASTER** is good too. These cost just a few dollars more a month and the teens can even pay for the ring master. Ring master allows your kids to give a number out to their friends and when they call, the phone will ring a certain way. This way you can tell if the phone is for you or your teens. Call waiting makes sure you never miss a call by beeping if you are already on the line. This is a must for emergencies.

THINGS I NEED TO DO TO ORGANIZE FAMILY COMMUNICATIONS
1. Buy FBB...
2. Get all kids' schedules...
3. Get carpool numbers...
4. Gather important phone numbers...
Fill in your own

4. ORGANIZE YOUR BATHROOMS

If you are like most families, chances are you might have more children than bathrooms. It is important to organize who uses what bathroom and when. A good timesaving tip for bigger families, especially one with several girls, (who hog every bathroom in total disregard for any rules) is to put a mirror in the kids' rooms so they can do make up, blow dry hair etc. in their own bedrooms without tying up the bathroom.

THINGS I NEED TO DO TO ORGANIZE THE BATHROOMS
1. Put mirror in each child's room.

5. ORGANIZE YOUR CLOSETS:

You realize that now that your son or daughter is in high school, it is imperative that he/she keep up on every fashion fad which comes along. If you are lucky, your high school has a uniform requirement. A few pointers which will make your life much easier is to teach your sons and daughters how to wash clothes and iron. Maybe have a domestic skills day where you show them how to cook a few things, iron, and in general, how to behave like perfect citizens. Never once in their high school years will they cause you even the slightest grief. Right?!

THINGS I NEED TO DO TO ORGANIZE THE CLOSETS
1. Check into baskets and shelves

6. ORGANIZE TRANSPORTATION.

Make sure you think about the transportation requirements of a high schooler's schedule. Set up a car pooling chart with who drives when and with phone numbers. Place the bus schedule here too, along with a taxi company's number. You and your spouse need to have a pre high school planning meeting to see which spouse can drive and when.

THINGS I NEED TO DO TO ORGANIZE THE TRANSPORTATION
1. Make lists of car pool members.

7. ORGANIZE YOUR RECORDS

If you have not started one already, start a high school file for your teen. Keep important records, and papers there. This is also a good place to keep a "clipping file". Anytime you see or read interesting articles dealing with important topics for your teen, clip them, and keep them in this file. They could be articles about summer camps, books, concerts, study techniques, drugs, anything that might benefit your high schooler. This file can be a great source for your next high schooler.

THINGS I NEED TO DO TO ORGANIZE MY RECORDS
1. Start high school clipping file.

8. ORGANIZE YOUR MONEY:

Obviously entire books have been written on this subject, so for us, we will just give you a pointer or two. Along with many new demands on time and energy, high school can put a lot of demands on finances. Be prepared for a multitude of additional expenses ranging from mechanical pencils to soccer shoes. A good thing to help reduce some of these additional expenses is to become active at the high school by helping kids organize fundraisers. Car washes, selling books, or recycling projects can help raise some extra money for supplies or activity costs.

If your teen has not already done so, he/she should be presenting you with the Money Saving Matching Contract found in Chapter 13. Read the contract over and if you have not done so already, help your high schooler set up a savings account in his/her name or jointly. You do not have to save a lot every month. It is just important that something goes into savings every month. Take this agreement very seriously. It is important to instill a consistent discipline when it comes to savings. Let them keep the savings book and make sure they know how to make deposits and withdrawals. Or maybe just deposits....

THINGS I NEED TO DO TO ORGANIZE MY MONEY
1. Start joint savings account.

9. MAKE A SCHEDULE:

Get yourself a nice weekly organizer and large monthly calendar for the new year. Post your family calendar on, you guessed it, your FBB (Family Bulletin Board).

Sit down with your high schooler(s) and review his or her school schedule. Your child will post his/her monthly and weekly schedule in his/her room on the bulletin board according to the super scheduling tips he/she received in Chapter 8. Read Chapter 8 and make a monthly and weekly personal schedule for yourself and the household. This will include meals, work schedules and chauffeuring activities such as car pooling and rides to work. Don't forget to review the school calendar usually found in the registration packet, in order to plan for holidays.

Also, do not forget to check if the activity or sport in which your child wants to participate starts before school. Some try outs actually start before the first day of classes.

Things I need to do to organize my schedule
1. *Write up monthly and weekly personal calendar.*

10. MAKE TIME TO STUDY WITH DESIGNATED FAMILY STUDY TIME ("FST"):

It is extremely important you set up a family study time. This means everyday, whether it is right after school or right after dinner, there will be at least an hour and a half of quiet; no TV, no phone calls, just study time. Discuss the time and the schedule with your teen and establish a study time for the whole family. Don't worry, you can schedule it around your favorite TV show. You can wait until school has been in a week and see what the best time is considering any practices, homework load and yes, even TV shows. During **FST (family study time)** try not to watch TV or talk on the phone. This is a quiet family time when the whole family is doing something productive. Use this time to read, pay bills, write a novel or do your own homework from work.

At the end of each night, check to see if your kids have finished their homework and have them tell you what they have done. If the kids do not have homework make them read a book or review old material instead. Be there for questions but never do their homework for them. Give kids the privacy they deserve, set up study/quiet reading times every day or evening.

Parents should get in the habit of quizzing their teens on occasion. Ask them about their studies and quiz them for any tests or memorization assignments. You should not do your child's homework but should assist as needed. Not only should you make sure your kids study, but check to see how they did on an assignment or quiz and praise or encourage them. Look through your teens' books also. See exactly what he/she will be learning. Sit down at the end of every month and ask your teen what is new.

GET INVOLVED

Research has have proven that children whose parents get involved in their education do better than children whose parents do not. It is that simple. Show your teen you are excited about his/her activities. Becoming involved with your child's education will lead to higher grades, higher self-esteem, more success for your child, at all of their endeavors, and a better home environment. It'll be a challenging 4 years but well worth your effort.

A FEW QUICK POINTERS TO REMEMBER ARE:

- 📖 Encourage your kids to read, especially the summer before high school starts.

- 📖 Encourage your teens to study and "get into" school.

- 📖 Encourage your child to participate in at least one extracurricular activity and do whatever it takes to set up car pooling for them.

- 📖 If your child does not make one team or activity, encourage him/her to try out for another.

HAVE AN EXTREMELY SERIOUS CONVERSATION WITH YOUR TEEN ABOUT THESE FOUR TOPICS:

- ❸ Talking to or taking rides from strangers.

- ❸ Sex, including abstinence and sexually transmitted diseases

- ❸ Drugs, including alcohol, pot, cocaine

- ❸ Safe driving

- ☻ Know the attendance policies of your child's school and reinforce the need to attend all classes.

- ☻ Try not to let problems disrupt your child's studying and concentration. Help keep problems at home from entering the classroom.

- ☻ Stay in contact with their high school advisor and teachers.

- ☻ Let your teens know they can call you at any time from any place for a ride home with no questions asked. Tell your teens not ever to get in a car when they know the driver has been drinking.

- ☻ Dating: Let your child know he/she is to tell you exactly where he/she is going. Let your kid's date know the exact curfew.

- ☻ Show your teens you have confidence in them and show an interest in whatever they do, whether it's flute lessons, soccer or sewing. Even if you do not understand why your child likes a particular activity, keep an open mind.

- ☻ Get him/her a grade school or junior high graduation gift. Watches, back packs, gift certificates, trips and/or do something special for him/her. Party, out for dinner etc.

- ☻ Think about your new high schooler.

This is a very important time for him/her, as I am sure you remember. Be there for him/her.

WHAT ARE SOME WAYS I CAN GET INVOLVED IN MY TEENS HIGH SCHOOL EDUCATION
1. Coach

WHEN SHOULD I START TO WORRY ABOUT COLLEGE AND MY FUTURE.

Believe it or not, right now! Once in high school make sure your teen has an academic check up every year to insure they are taking all of the necessary classes for high school graduation and college admissions. Your child's counselor or academic advisor will help. Your child does not want to end up in his/her senior year in high school not being able to graduate with his/her friends because he/she forgot to take one class. Think about having him/her around the house under those circumstances!!

REMEMBER COLLEGE ADMISSIONS LOOK AT 5 FACTORS WHEN DECIDING ON LETTING STUDENTS IN:

1. How hard are the classes they took in high school?

2. Rank in class/Grade Point Average

3. SAT-I or ACT test scores.

4. Counselor/teacher recommendations.

5. Activities in and out of school.

Be supportive and interested in their college and career preparation activities. Take your teen to work for a day, on field trips and talk to him/her about his/her future. Let your teen dream and provide him/her with all the information he/she needs so they can dream accurately. Let him/her discover things by trying out various activities. Make sure your teen is using the counselors and advisors to the maximum and visiting with them at least once or twice a semester, especially for the academic health check up. Encourage your teen to take more challenging classes. This helps him/her get into college. Talk to your kid about what high school activities he/she should participate in to prepare for college. Counseling offices have computer programs, videos, magazines and books which assist you in getting ready for and selecting a college. *THE GREATEST BOOK IN THE ENTIRE WORLD FOR THIS TOPIC IS* How to get into and graduate from college in 4 years with good grades, a useful major, a lot of knowledge, a little debt, great friends, happy parents, maximum party attendance, minimal weight gain, decent habits, fewer hassles, a career goal and a super attitude, all while remaining extremely cool! *BY GUESS WHO, MARTIN SPETHMAN.*

Remember also, college is not free. You should definitely start saving now if you have not done so already. Two investment firms that will provide you with some useful college financial planning kits are:

T. Rowe Price
Offers a free step-by-step college financial planning kit. To order one call (800) 638-5660.

Liberty Financial Companies, Inc
Offers a free step-by-step college financial planning kit. To order one call (617)-722-6000

CONGRATULATIONS, now you are ready for high school....again!!

Be sure to first check with the college/career office at your child's high school. They have a tremendous amount of free material on college and career planning, including information on financial planning.

ADDRESSES AND PHONE NUMBERS:

Name   Phone #

Address

Last words of wisdom

Name   Phone #

Address

Last words of wisdom

Name   Phone #

Address

Last words of wisdom

Name   Phone #

Address

Last words of wisdom

Name   Phone #

Address

Last words of wisdom

Name   Phone #

Address

Last words of wisdom

ADDRESSES AND PHONE NUMBERS:

Name   Phone #

Address

Last words of wisdom

Name   Phone #

Address

Last words of wisdom

Name   Phone #

Address

Last words of wisdom

Name   Phone #

Address

Last words of wisdom

Name   Phone #

Address

Last words of wisdom

Name   Phone #

Address

Last words of wisdom

ADDRESSES AND PHONE NUMBERS:

Name   Phone #

Address

Last words of wisdom

Name   Phone #

Address

Last words of wisdom

Name   Phone #

Address

Last words of wisdom

Name   Phone #

Address

Last words of wisdom

Name   Phone #

Address

Last words of wisdom

Name   Phone #

Address

Last words of wisdom